CAMBRIDGE LIBRARY COLLECTION

Books of enduring scholarly value

Polar Exploration

This series includes accounts, by eye-witnesses and contemporaries, of early expeditions to the Arctic and the Antarctic. Huge resources were invested in such endeavours, particularly the search for the North-West Passage, which, if successful, promised enormous strategic and commercial rewards. Cartographers and scientists travelled with many of the expeditions, and their work made important contributions to earth sciences, climatology, botany and zoology. They also brought back anthropological information about the indigenous peoples of the Arctic region and the southern fringes of the American continent. The series further includes dramatic and poignant accounts of the harsh realities of working in extreme conditions and utter isolation in bygone centuries.

Reflections on the Mysterious Fate of Sir John Franklin

The disappearance of Sir John Franklin's Arctic expedition of 1845 led to many rescue attempts, some by the British government and some by private individuals, as well as a large number of works recounting these expeditions and reflecting on the mystery. Little is known about the author of this 1857 work, James Parsons. He begins this dramatic account by noting that the disappearance of a large and well-equipped party is almost unprecedented in the Arctic: nothing certain was known about Franklin's fate twelve years after the last recorded sighting. Parsons' speculations derive from a knowledge of naval practice, and familiarity with the seas and climate of the Arctic region and the records of earlier expeditions. He offers practical suggestions about a new attempt using steam-boats, but knows that this will be to find out what actually happened, because there could now be no possibility of finding survivors.

T0371213

Cambridge University Press has long been a pioneer in the reissuing of out-of-print titles from its own backlist, producing digital reprints of books that are still sought after by scholars and students but could not be reprinted economically using traditional technology. The Cambridge Library Collection extends this activity to a wider range of books which are still of importance to researchers and professionals, either for the source material they contain, or as landmarks in the history of their academic discipline.

Drawing from the world-renowned collections in the Cambridge University Library and other partner libraries, and guided by the advice of experts in each subject area, Cambridge University Press is using state-of-the-art scanning machines in its own Printing House to capture the content of each book selected for inclusion. The files are processed to give a consistently clear, crisp image, and the books finished to the high quality standard for which the Press is recognised around the world. The latest print-on-demand technology ensures that the books will remain available indefinitely, and that orders for single or multiple copies can quickly be supplied.

The Cambridge Library Collection brings back to life books of enduring scholarly value (including out-of-copyright works originally issued by other publishers) across a wide range of disciplines in the humanities and social sciences and in science and technology.

Reflections on the Mysterious Fate of Sir John Franklin

JAMES PARSONS

CAMBRIDGE
UNIVERSITY PRESS

University Printing House, Cambridge, CB2 8BS, United Kingdom

Cambridge University Press is part of the University of Cambridge.
It furthers the University's mission by disseminating knowledge in the pursuit of
education, learning and research at the highest international levels of excellence.

www.cambridge.org
Information on this title: www.cambridge.org/9781108072052

© in this compilation Cambridge University Press 2014

This edition first published 1857
This digitally printed version 2014

ISBN 978-1-108-07205-2 Paperback

This book reproduces the text of the original edition. The content and language reflect
the beliefs, practices and terminology of their time, and have not been updated.

Cambridge University Press wishes to make clear that the book, unless originally published
by Cambridge, is not being republished by, in association or collaboration with,
or with the endorsement or approval of, the original publisher or its successors in title.

REFLECTIONS

ON

THE MYSTERIOUS FATE

OF

SIR JOHN FRANKLIN.

BY

JAMES PARSONS.

LONDON:

J. F. HOPE, 16 GREAT MARLBOROUGH STREET.

1857.

INTRODUCTION.

IT must be a subject of great interest to all classes, when in this enlightened age an expedition like that under Sir John Franklin, leaves the shores of Great Britain and is lost in a manner so complete as to frustrate every attempt to dispel the darkness that enshrouds its fate, and to hold at defiance the combined talents of the civilized world. In the records of past ages we find but two expeditions lost while on Arctic discovery, one commanded by Sir Hugh Willoughby in 1554, on the northern coast of Lapland, and the other under Messrs Knight and Barlow in 1719, on Marble Island, Hudson's Bay. Yet in the absence of a search the fate of Willoughby was made known two years after he sailed, that of Messrs. Knight and Barlow before ten years had expired. In what form can be compared either of those expeditions to that now absent twelve years? They may be instanced to show that history does not furnish a parallel, but they will bear no comparison with Sir John Franklin's. For what expedition ever sailed with so large a number of experienced men, so many scientific acquirements, and with such sanguine hopes, as that of 1845 ? What search was ever so great or so barren as the search for it has been ? Expectations have sprung up concerning it but to vanish as suddenly as they were formed. An extensive capital has been expended for a purpose still to be revealed. When the force of science with the benefit of experience could not prevail, the inexperienced placed their views of the mystery beside those of navigators, and met alike the same degree of disappointment. Such has been the fact, and such the forlorn results attained throughout a period of the past ten years.

JAMES PARSONS.

27, *Duke Street,*
North Shields, Northumberland.
February 19, 1857.

MYSTERIOUS FATE

SIR JOHN FRANKLIN.

————◆————

As it is not generally known, whether Sir John Franklin had with him on leaving Whale Fish Islands in July, 1845, an Esquimaux and dogs, the veil of mystery first appears in this vicinity. With stores and a full allowance of provisions for three years, he sailed for Melville Bay, and a passage through the middle ice into Lancaster Sound; previous to reaching that bay, he threw overboard an Admiralty cylinder, which was found by the Lady Jane, whaler, in 1849— thus showing that he had obeyed an interesting part of his instructions. On the 26th of July, the Prince of Wales, whaler, met the expedition moored to an iceberg in latitude 74-48 north, longitude, 66-13 west, it was then waiting a favourable opening through the middle ice to proceed onwards to Lancaster Sound. This is the last time it was seen by Europeans. Having arrived in Barrow's Strait, Franklin would push direct for Cape Walker. Being unable to reach it for ice, and finding Peel Sound blocked up, he would naturally proceed northward to the entrance of Wellington Channel, and make Erebus and Terror Bay his first winter quarters. Remaining here until the summer of '46, he passed into unknown waters, to discover, if possible, the north west passage. Here an important question presents itself—did Franklin leave a despatch on Beechey Island, previous to his departure in 1846. None such have been found, was he so far lost to the safety of his men, as to neglect leaving a despatch either here or at Cape Walker ? It is highly improbable, as in his former voyages he always left despatches where they were deemed necessary. It is contrary to reason to imagine that he attempted the route by Cape Walker without leaving some written document, and after being foiled in that attempt, turned his ships to Beechey Island and Wellington Channel without leaving a notice of his proceedings. Doubtless, he had good reasons for altering his course from Cape Walker to Beechey Island, though no motive can be shown why, after attempting both routes, he left no despatches at either. Being convinced he left despatches at Beechey Island in 1846, how they have disappeared, is a question to be touched upon in another portion of my views. The caution of Franklin is at once seen in the selection of Erebus and Terror Bay as his winter quarters—the very shape and position of which giving him perfect security from danger, it being much broader within than at its entrance. The ice must break up before the ships could be carried out into Barrow Strait, and when that took place the screws of the missing ships would soon clear them of loose ice. All the heavy ice coming down Wellington Channel and Barrow Strait would pass by the ships, instead of carrying them helplessly away as were the ships of Sir James Ross, and those of the American expedition. In the Autumn of 1846, the missing expedition has cut itself out of Erebus and Terror Bay, a task in which great assistance would be rendered by the screws of the ships, and fixing a trustworthy period in the month of August, it left Beechey Island, and took its way north through Wellington Channel for the western entrance of Jones' Sound, in the hope of proving its connection with that channel. Having discovered its junction, Franklin would naturally explore it,

and by directing a party eastward accomplish his
object, after which he would deposit, as an act
of prudence, some provisions in caches near
the turning point of Wellington Channel, in the
event of having to retreat by the way he advanced, and for the information of parties in
search, he would leave a despatch stating his
intentions and discoveries. It is clear that his
first attention after passing up Wellington
Channel would be fixed on the western entrance
of Jones' Sound, the importance attached to
it being so great that a passage by that route
was not only conjectured before he sailed, but
was named the eastern entrance of the great
Polar passage; Franklin, therefore, knowing its
importance, would strive to effect its exploration, and by circumstances hereafter to be named
he must have done so, now seeing the Victoria
Islands beyond him to the north, he would shape
his course between them and Parry's Islands.

It is requisite here to mention three circumstances that would materially assist in carrying him onwards in his adventurous path.
First throughout the season of '46 there prevailed strong north easterly gales, which rendered
it a disastrous season to the whalers; the second
is the existence of a current running westward
to the north of Cape Lady Franklin. And again,
the missing ships were fitted with the screw
propeller, which could if necessary render essen-
tial service. They were unlike other ships

sent in search, one towing another. The lost
ships could act independently of each other, thus
giving them great advantages. With these
powerful circumstances in favour of their course,
and being in sight of unknown lands, the spirits
of the whole expedition would be aroused,—here
the bold daring of the gallant Franklin would sti-
mulate them to pursue their course to the lands
in view, and to others far beyond. While the
route was open they would persevere to
the westward until the season of '46 had
closed.

The summer of '47 having arrived they may
have gone somewhat further in the hope of completing the passage, but have been again stopped
by the heavy Polar ice, and the north easterly set of
the current through Behring's Strait ; yet as so
much progress had been made in '46 those difficulties would appear but trifling compared with
the success. Franklin would then with parties
explore the lands around his ships, and looking
upon his position (debarring its isolated nature)
in the same light as that of Captain Mc Clure
in 1850—51, I conclude he ran the full length
of his discoveries with the ships in the extraordinary season of '46. Captain Mc Clure effected
his achievements in the favourable seasons of
'50—51, and though he had remained near his
first winter quarters three years, he made no
progress eastward with his ship, and finally had
to abandon her to her fate. As the open season

of '51 allowed her to visit Mercy Bay, it will require another such season for her release, lying as she does on the north coast of a land wedged in by the pressure of the heavy northern ice. Such a season may prevail several years running, or it may appear once in twenty years.

Conceiving the missing ships to be ice-locked in a Strait or Harbour to the north and west of Parry's Islands, we leave Franklin to push forward his discoveries, and turn anxiously towards that part of his instructions bearing on his route, and as it is said by going up Wellington Channel he attached greater importance to his own opinions than to the experience and views of others, it will be well (previous to reviewing his instructions) to speak of the motives which led that great man to prefer the northern course to that by Cape Walker and Peel Sound; they were the hope of finding a clear passage through Wellington Channel, and from it the western entrance of Jones' Sound, the expectation of an open Polar Sea northward of Parry's Island, and the discovery of the north west passage as was conjectured before he sailed. He knew when Wellington Channel was discovered it was ice free, and he must have reasonably anticipated by going north that a large field lay open for discovery. These then are the motives that led him to choose the northern route before that by Cape Walker:

nor shall we varnish his character by saying it
every way suited his well known zeal for discovery.   Whereas, by Cape Walker, the difficulties appeared both great and numerous ; there
was a belief that a group of islands existed south
west of that Cape, together with the ice drifting
towards Coronation Gulf, an absence of open
water, and the presence of a small but dangerous
field for discovery.   He was well aware of the
voyage of Sir Edward Parry in 1819 to Melville
Island, and that gallant officer's long and hopeless detention at Winter Harbour.   By the un-
favourable prospects presented in 1819 south
and west of that island, he beheld at once the
impossibility of pushing vessels in that direction.
How far this prediction of difficulties has been
verified, we have unmistakable evidence in the
voyages of Captains Mc Clure and Collinson
from   the   west, and   in   those   of Captains
Austin and Kellet from the east.   Two ships
were lost in the attempt from the east, and one
in that from the west, nor were they proved by
the experience of a season or by one route, but
through several seasons and by different routes,
leaving us, in fine, nothing to record but the fatal
results of attempting to push ships through a
path which Franklin was desirous of avoid-
ing.
    From the motives that led him to prefer the
northern route, we pass to the instructions given
him by the Admiralty, the most interesting part

of which runs thus : " Lancaster Sound and its continuation through Barrow Strait having been four times navigated by Sir Edward Parry, and since by whaling ships, will probably be found without any obstacles from ice or islands, and Sir Edward Parry having also proceeded from the latter in a straight course to Melville Island, it is hoped that the remaining portion of the passage, about 900 miles to Behring's Strait, may also be found equally free from obstructions, and in proceeding to the westward, therefore, you will not stop to examine any openings either to the northward or southward in that Strait, but continue to push to the westward without loss of time in the latitude of about seventy-four and a quarter till you have reached the longitude of that portion of land on which Cape Walker is situated. From that point we desire that every effort be used to endeavour to penetrate to the southward and westward, in a course as direct towards Behring's Strait as the position and extent of the ice or the existence of land may admit ; but should your progress be arrested by ice of a permanent appearance, and that when passing the mouth of the strait between Devon and Cornwallis Islands you had observed that it was open, and clear of ice, we desire that you will duly consider whether that channel might not offer a more practicable outlet from the Archipelago, and a more ready access to the open sea."

This concluding passage, although so clear
and powerful, seems to have escaped the attention of those fully aware of its existence. No
impartial mind can dwell thereon without
concluding Franklin would have disobeyed his
instructions by going south west of Cape
Walker. Because he then would have been
running into the difficulties of which they
particularly warned him. The anticipation
of meeting ice of a permanent appearance
whilst entangled amidst a group of islands,
must act with marvellous effect upon the
mind of a man having two routes to choose
from. If the Lords of the Admiralty wished
Franklin to pay attention to the route by Cape
Walker, why depict in his instructions the probability of meeting ice of a permanent appearance, and likewise an Archipelago in that direction? While, had they been desirous that he
should abolish the idea of going up Wellington
Channel, why did they say, if in passing its entrance you observe it open and clear of ice, we
desire that you will duly consider, whether it
might not offer a more practicable outlet from
the Archipelago, and a more ready access to the
open sea. The probability of finding Wellington
Channel clear of ice and the temptation of an
open sea northward, should not have been held
out to Franklin, if their Lordships did not wish
him to attempt that route. Is the scene not
one of horror, in beholding a man running his

ships amidst an Archipelago to be ensnared with ice of a permanent appearance. What navigator would make the attempt? Where is the man who would not use every exertion to avoid such a difficult and dangerous path as Franklin's instructions pourtrayed in the route by Cape Walker? Had he declared his intention of struggling for the passage south-west of that cape, and the Admiralty wished him to abandon the attempt, they could not have figured greater difficulties and dangers to lead him from his determination than they did in the instructions under which he sailed. Therefore, in pushing south-west of Cape Walker, he would not only be running into the dangers of which Dr. King especially forewarned him, but into those very difficulties which his instructions clearly revealed to his notice. By following the northern course he acted in every way up to the tenor of his orders; where then arose the sanguine opinion (and unlimited confidence attached thereto) reposed in the minds of the many, that according to his instructions, Franklin must have gone south-west of Cape Walker with his ships in the season of '46. It is in vain we search for its foundation. If others are cognizant of its source I assuredly confess my ignorance of its existence. It is no pleasant task to add that the majority of those officers who gave their opinions on the position of the missing ships, remained firm towards the route by Cape Walker in opposition

and directly in the face of the orders Franklin
received to the contrary. That brief passage
deserved the attention of all who felt interested
in his behalf, instead of receiving, as it did, the
insulting silence of the whole community. Its
importance was as great as it proved fatal, because
it was the index to a route offering (at the time
the lost expedition sailed) the least difficulties
to its progress. Here the want of consideration
is painfully felt, nor can its absence be more
plainly observed, than in the present clouded and
forlorn state of the mystery. Little credit is due
to the experienced, when one who disowns he
ever crossed the Arctic Circle is, through the
helpless state of the subject, compelled to draw
public attention to facts connected therewith,
as clear as noon-day, and as simple as they are
clear. After they have been so long neglected,
and still receive nothing from the world but an
ignominious silence, I cannot but exclaim, we
live in a wonderful age, when the most vital
parts of a question of such great importance are
treated with a strict and scornful silence, while
subjects bordering on the confines of folly, rivet
the attention of all not only when in dispute
but long after they have been placed beyond
doubt.

And now returning to Franklin's position in
the distant north, where, after pushing his explorations to their utmost limits in the season of
'47, he passes the winter and awaits the turn of

'48 in the expectation of a more favourable season. The autumn of that year having arrived without releasing the ships, it has made their position critical, he would now see there was no time to be lost; the vast resources of his memory would be called into action for the relief of his men, and at this period, that truly unfortunate but heroic navigator's efforts have been centred in a retreat unsurpassed in the annals of discovery. In a bold attempt so illustrative of his daring character, it is evident he would after '48 trust to the good fortune of the seasons no longer, as the treachery of the previous seasons showed there could be no reliance placed on them, he would thereby adopt such means as he thought requisite for getting communication or retreating to where succour was to be found, consequently, he would despatch a powerful boat party, as soon as the spring of '49 set in, to communicate with searching parties at Wellington Channel, or at Beechey Island, where he would certainly expect either ships or parties to be found. In making a retreat at the stated period, he did not heedlessly endanger the lives of his men by delay; the danger arose from obstacles and not altogether from a long imprisonment, as when he reached his second winter quarters (say October '46,) two years had but expired when he determined on a retreat; he could persevere those two years for the passage; when on half allowance his provisions would serve until the autumn of

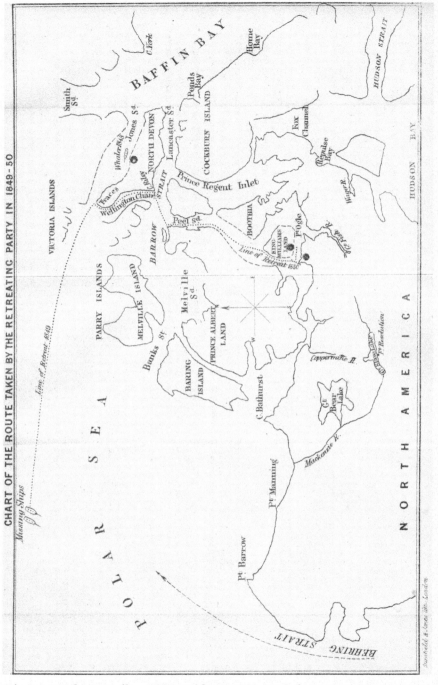

CHART OF THE ROUTE TAKEN BY THE RETREATING PARTY IN 1849-50

The material originally positioned here is too large for reproduction in this reissue. A PDF can be downloaded from the web address given on page iv of this book, by clicking on 'Resources Available'.

50. When the retreating party left, he calcu-
lated on having eighteen or twenty months
provisions to serve on half allowance, until relief
was sent by that party, therefore he cannot be
charged with any reckless hazard of his men.
The loss of the ships must be attributed to the
treachery of the seasons, but the loss of life to
the absence of relief at Beechey Island and Cape
Walker in '49-50. The favourable season to
them of '46, and the assisting circumstances
already named, betrayed those brave men. The
aid of their zeal was not wanted to carry them
onwards to their doom. But in the warmth of
success they gave way to an impulse natural to
their race, and in a daring attempt to retrieve
their misfortune, like martyrs suffered, and like
heroes died. When the spring of '49 arrived,
Franklin having previously organized a party,
would despatch it first to retreat on the stores
left in '46 (while on his way north) near the
junction of Jones' Sound with Wellington Channel,
and if no ships or intelligence were there, it could
push down Wellington Channel to Beechey
Island, where ships or searching parties were sure
to be found. It is beyond the power of my pen
to describe the farewell accompanying the outset
of the retreating party. But the cheer, the last
adieu, the prayer of hope, and the anxious
lingering gaze of the remaining men as the
gallant band took its desolate way across the
distant horizon, come vividly before us. To

follow its footsteps after leaving the ships is a
task by no means difficult. It would make the
best possible use of the season of '49, yet having
a great distance to travel, with the ice and current
to contend against, the season would be severely
diminished when it made the western entrance
of Jones' Sound. Having arrived at the stores,
they would set watch for ships coming up
Wellington Channel, and if disappointed in seeing any, they would remove the despatch left
near the stores in '46, finding it untouched and
no trace whatever of a searching party, they
would conclude that a search had not been made
in that direction. Their strongest hopes now
fix on Beechey Island, and after emptying the
caches of their contents have made all haste down
Wellington Channel to that island, expecting
every hour to meet ships or searching parties,
but they have reached it and found none.

A fact may now be related that will account
for no trace of them being found on the shores
of Wellington Channel by the searching parties,
in '50. It is well known that on the 1st of
September '49, large bodies of ice came down
Barrow Strait and Wellington Channel, and in its
impetuous course carried the expedition under
Sir James Ross away from the entrance of the
latter eastward through Lancaster Sound, and
as far south as Pond's Bay before it escaped from
its perilous position. As some of those masses
came down Wellington Channel with the wes-

terly gales at that time prevalent, that channel must have been left ice free. And this remarkable incident happening at the very time Franklin's men were near its northern entrance would allow them to retreat southward in clear water. Hence the absence of traces on the shores of Wellington Channel in 1850. It is a very doubtful question whether they could have reached the western entrance of Jones' Sound, in the season of '49, had they not been favoured by this eruption of the ice caused by the westerly gales, which proved to them more fatal than otherwise, for although they wonderfully assisted their journey eastward, they were extremely fatal in carrying the relief expedition under Sir James Ross from the south entrance of Wellington Channel, when those unfortunate men were so near and so much required assistance. After reaching Beechey Island they must have been woefully disappointed in not finding ships, and as the season was past for the whalers, escape by them was hopeless, they would scan the adjoining headlands for marks or signals. But, ill-fated men, it was in vain they looked in every direction for some object to reward them, but desolation everywhere met their view. Little suspecting such negligence possible, they would search the whole neighbourhood for cairns, or traces of a searching party. But to their horror, and to England's eternal shame, they found not a trace or mark of any description left. Not even a stone

was there to show those gallant men they had
ever once been searched for ; and to be fully convinced of the painful truth, they have gone to
the despatches left by themselves in '46, and
which are now missing. Here they have found
them alone and untouched. Where then lay
their hopes of succour ? What indeed was their
thoughts of the country that sent them ? As
any attempt to describe their feelings when
seeing themselves thus forsaken, will meet with
certain failure, I refrain from the attempt. But
while this simple view justly answers the absence
of despatches from Beechey Island, it may be
asked, why after removing them they did not
leave others, to which reason answers the fact
of men returning and finding despatches untouched that were deposited by them four years
previous to retreat is, in the absence of further
hope, a substantial reason for not leaving others
in their place. When despatches are left at places
those who deposit them expect they will be found,
but when that belief is destroyed, how can we
hope to find others. After Franklin's party had
been five years on a dangerous voyage and had
visited places in retreat, where ships ought to
have been two years and a half previous to that
time, what hope could they entertain of succour
from ships ? When such interesting places as
Jones' Sound and the south entrance of Wellington Channel remained throughout a space of
five years unvisited.—I should be delighted to

learn the advantages they could expect by leaving another despatch at Beechey Island. It is evident that if the least ray of hope possessed the party after its arrival at that island, it would concentrate on Cape Walker, as it was the first place Franklin's instructions led him to visit. Closing here on the mystery of the absent despatches, we are attracted towards the critical position of the party while at Beechey Island; the officers (as Franklin was not there,) had urgent matters to decide upon, the past was dreadful, yet the future appeared worse. The main question for their consideration was the course they were to pursue. From their present position two routes appeared, that by Cape Walker and Peel Sound for the continent of America, and the Hudson's Bay Company's settlements, and eastward through Barrow Strait in search of whalers.

Let us give this question strict attention, for it stands boldly to view; why did they prefer retreat by Cape Walker and Peel Sound to that by Barrow Strait? In favour of the former was a faint hope of ships or intelligence at that cape; an expectation of meeting Esquimaux near the continent, from whom assistance in travelling might be obtained; a strong belief that information could be derived from those tribes regarding any searching parties; and by reaching the continent it was possible to send intelligence of their position and wants to the Hudson's Bay Company's settlements; a good prospect of reaching the hunting grounds in summer to kill deer, and by making them the half-way post between Cape Walker and the settlements on Great Slave Lake, communication, that great object, would be established : when they found no search had been made for them in Barrow Strait, they would naturally expect it was going on from the continent ; could they imagine England sent them on that desperate undertaking and left them destitute in the hour of need ? Here is a weighty combination of reasons why the officers of the party gave preference to the route by Peel Sound instead of Barrow Strait. Glancing at the latter we observe many obstacles therein presented, which in attempting to push eastward were impossible to surmount. There was no hope of meeting whalers, and as little chance of finding Esquimaux ; no settlements appeared without travelling seven or eight hundred miles, and that also across the heavy ice in Baffin's Bay : no hunting grounds were in view, nor any prospect of getting communication. The only point short of impossibility was the chance of meeting whalers, and when the season of 1850 had commenced the long period they had to survive and the risk attending that journey were too great to sacrifice. The lives of the remaining men depended on their success ; therefore they could not wait till the month of August on the mere chance of meeting a whaler. By self experience they knew that Lancaster

Sound could not be entered by those ships until that period of the season, and was not by themselves (though assisted by steam) until that month, and then arose the reflection that Lancaster Sound in those years as at present was seldom visited by whalers at any part of the season. The number of ships fishing in those seas being so few that many years pass over without their effecting an entrance into that passage; Franklin while on his way to the North in '45 had a powerful instance of this, when throughout the whole passage he met but two whalers and those near the east coast of Baffin's Bay on the 26th of July; again H. M. S. Phœnix in 1854, under Captain Inglefield, navigated Baffin's Bay, east west, north and south, meeting after all but five whalers near Home Bay, three hundred miles south-east of Lancaster Sound. The same vessel left Disco Island, latitude 70 north, longitude 55 west, August 7th, '54, and running up Baffin's Bay passed through the middle ice into Lancaster Sound, after visiting Beechey Island returned and put into Pond's Bay, the seat of the whale fishery, crossing again to Disco Island, she steamed southward and doubled Cape Farewell, making a run of near two thousand miles through the heart of the fishery without meeting a whaler. Still further, Dr. Kane traversed the northern shores of Baffin's Bay two seasons '54—55, and could not find a whaler to relieve him. Should conviction

still remain stubborn, another instance is seen
in the escape of Sir John Ross, who visited the
south shore of Barrow Strait twice in search of
whalers (once in 1832, and again in August '33)
when he fortunately met the Isabella of Hull,
in which vessel he returned to England ; this
event be it remembered occurred at a period when
hundreds of ships navigated those seas and
penetrated into parts unseen at the present time,
yet withal it was termed a miraculous escape.
The chances of success in 1850 were therefore too
slender to warrant Franklin's party making an
attempt, while to reach Uppernavic (the nearest
Danish settlement) by crossing the packed ice
in Baffin's and Melville Bays would be a task
beyond conception ; such an attempt would not
only meet death, but would do so without the
slightest hope of discovering its unfortunate
victims.   They were kept in ignorance of any
depôt being in Barrow Strait, and had they
effected a retreat to the eastward along its
northern shore, they would have found no depot,
as they were all made on that of its southern.
In reviewing the difficulties against a retreat by
Barrow Strait and the advantages to be derived
by an attempt through Peel Sound, what
course appeared so favourable as that of the
latter. Between the difficulties and dangers on
one hand, and the benefits likely to arise on the
other, could they have selected a route better
adapted for the emergency than the one they

have followed; with so many advantages in its
favour and being the only direct road from
Barrow Strait to the continent? We may place
every confidence that Peel Sound was the
channel Franklin's party took to seek communication after quitting Beechey Island.

But in the dawn of 1850 calamities of an
awful description await that brave band of men ;
after meeting naught but disappointment and
neglect where they expected succour, they are
compelled through want and in faith to their
companions to leave Beechey Island.   Early in
the season of '50 they left it, and directed their
steps towards Cape Walker, to ascertain whether
ships or intelligence had arrived there.   Having
approached it, and seen no marks or signals left
by searching parties, they may have landed, but
as at Beechey Island, found no trace of any to
reward them ; then convinced that no ships had
been on search, they, with scarcely a stop-
page, as time was important, and having their
country's cruelty at heart, are driven as a
last resource to attempt a passage to the
Hudson's Bay Company's settlements.   The
struggle now becomes one of life and death.
They know that they must not only suffer
themselves, but the lives of their companions
depend on their success.   They would therefore use every exertion, strain every nerve to
arrive at a speedy communication with the settlements, and to effect this object, have selected the

passage by Peel Sound in preference to the route by Barrow Strait, the absence of ships or intelligence from Beechey Island and Cape Walker, between the seasons of '49-'50, having reduced them to the melancholy extreme of selling their lives as dearly as possible by attempting the settlements, or to miserably perish in the forlorn attempt. From Cape Walker they would make a retreat south, through Peel Sound, travelling near its western shore, and finding that passage blocked with hummocky field ice, as Sir James Ross found it in June, '49, their progress would become slow and difficult, their enfeebled condition greatly prolonging their journey to the continent. Keeping these circumstances, therefore, in mind, it is but reasonable to conclude that it would be in the spring of '50 when they arrived at the north coast of King William's Land. That this was the case may be inferred from the Esquimaux narrative brought to England in '54 by Dr. Rae, namely, " That in the spring of '50, while some Esquimaux were killing seals near the northern coast of King William's Land, a party of about forty white men appeared, dragging a boat over the ice from the north. They stated their ships had been crushed in the ice, and they were now going to the hunting grounds to shoot deer; the men looked thin (as well they might), and purchased a seal from the natives. At a later date of the same season, but previous to the breaking up of the ice, the dead bodies of thirty were found on the mainland and five on an island near it, about a long day's journey to the north west of a large stream, said to be the Great Fish River.   After this statement the mind is impressed by the reflection that during the interval of twelve months which elapsed from September 1st, 1849, when Sir James Ross was driven out of Barrow's Strait, until August 23rd, 1850, when Captain Austin's expedition arrived at Beechey Island, no ship or party was on search in Barrow Strait.   Within this period the faithful companions of Sir John Franklin were seeking that help so long denied them by their country, a remnant of the gallant crew was then in retreat for life and liberty, a retreat which gives to their mysterious fate the semblance of a tragedy ; and when comparing that fatal interval with the absence of despatches from Beechey Island, and with the period at which the Esquimaux saw the party on the north coast of King William's Land, we are drawn away helplessly into the workings of the mystery.

Having now explained the course taken by Franklin in '46 and the retreat of his party in '49—'50 we proceed to more fully confirm those views by a chain of circumstances which for breadth, simplicity, and power is seldom surpassed. The main points of retreat are seen by the traces found in the autumn of 1850 on Beechey Island and Cape Riley, as well as by those discovered in 1853 near the western entrance of Jones' Sound.

The former traces were discovered but a few months after the retreating party had left, and consisted of two tame Esquimaux dogs, part of a trisail of one of the missing ships, several remnants of clothing, patched and worn threadbare in every direction, a few strips of paper laying quite exposed, one bearing the handwriting of Commander Fitzjames, and another the name of Mr. McDonald, assistant surgeon of the Terror. And on Cape Riley were seen marks of five tents having been pitched, the stones being left that had kept down the canvass.

We commence first with the dogs found by the American Expedition, and as there is no Esquimaux within several hundred miles of Beechey Island, to whom had they belonged, and how long could they have been on that island when found? Being tame, is a sufficient proof that they had been with Esquimaux or white men. The absence of the former from Barrow Strait proves that the dogs did not belong to them, and had they been a lengthy period on Beechey Island they would not have been tame. Franklin would not leave dogs on that island in 1846, knowing too well their value in travelling, and if he did, would they not be wild in the autumn of 1850? I conclude, therefore, that the retreating party carried them down Wellington Channel in '49, and being too weak to proceed further have left them when quitting Beechey Island for Cape Walker, to exist on the bones and remains near the place where they were found. Their identity could have been proved if Franklin had purchased dogs at Whale Fish Islands in '45, as by taking them back to the parties from whom he bought them, they would immediately have recognized them if they were the same.

What decision can we form in finding part of a trisail of either of the ships cut into the shape of a tent-top—could this have been done in '46? To cut up any of the sails of his ships, would be an experiment too hazardous for Franklin to adopt at the very time he required all their assistance. Besides, he had plenty of good tents in '46, and at Beechey Island he had met with no casualty that could reduce him to that great necessity; a party in retreat four years afterwards would probably have tents made of the ship's sails, as those taken with them from England, would, if much in use, be worn out. When compelled by necessity to cut up the sails of his ships for tents, Franklin must have thought more of hunting, or a retreat by his boats, than an escape by his ships.

The *Illustrated London News*, October 4th, 1851, when reviewing the traces found in '50, thus speaks of the clothing :—" A few remnants of clothing brought over denote the situation of the wearer to have been deplorable. They consist of a pair of seaman's trousers, which must have been worn long after the buttons had ceased to be of use. They are mended in all possible directions, and evidently patched with what had once been thick flannel, but worn until not a vestige of nap remained, and even in many places worn completely through. A pair of drawers and a few stockings were found much in the same condition. A portion of a shirt, forming the back part of the neck, collar, and back, from the fineness of the linen had most likely belonged to one of the officers." From whence springs this state of wretchedness? Did this period overtake them while at Beechey Island in '46, and before they had been fifteen months from England? And would Franklin have pushed his adventurous way into the unknown world after his crews had reached this high stage of destitution. It is needless to question, when the presence of the retreating party in '50 already replies. In rotation we follow the strips of paper bearing the handwriting of Commander Fitzjames, and the name of McDonald. There is a power in this trace which does not appear at first sight. It is—Could they have lain from the summer of '46, when the expedition departed, until the autumn of '50, when they were found.

Without a despatch-tin or a shelter of any description to preserve them from the weather, is it possible they could exist after four years' exposure to all the rigours of that fearful climate, when such durable articles as coal-sacks, rope, canvass, &c., are bleached and rotted in a

season or two? How could the frail material
of paper exist after four years' exposure, and
still distinctly show the handwriting of him who
had written thereon? It seems utterly impossible. From the handwriting of Commander Fitzjames being found, coupled with his
daring character, nothing is more likely than
that he had either accompanied or commanded
the retreating party, he being such an officer as Franklin would select for such a
duty. The last, but most important trace
connected with the vicinity of Beechey Island,
is the five tent marks on Cape Riley, which
proves that a large party had been there. Now
for what object was it sent there? It could
not have been for a sporting purpose while the
ships lay at that island in '45-'46, as a party
leaving the ships for sport on Cape Riley would
not require five tents, the distance to and from
the vessels being so short, that the object in
view would not have repaid the labour of carrying them up to its summit. Moreover, had it
been a party sent in pursuit of any scientific
purpose, what use could it have for five tents?
If Franklin sent a party upon Cape Riley
previous to his departure in '46, it would be to
watch the ice moving down Barrow Strait, a
duty which two men from the ships, relieved
every watch, could easily have accomplished.
Taking all these things into consideration, our
verdict, therefore, is that those tent marks were

left by the retreating party in '49—'50. The Esquimaux narrative says that some of their bodies were found in tents. Now would not the five tents pitched on Cape Riley just accommodate such a party as that seen by the Esquimaux? Their object by encamping thereon was to watch for any searching parties traversing the ice to the south-east, while its prominent position enabled them to explore the headlands eastward, for marks or cairns that may have been left.

When the opening meeting of the Royal Geographical Society in 1855 took place, Sir John Ross stated that an empty despatch-tin was found on or near Beechey Island by the searching parties of '50, a circumstance needless of further explanation, as it simply confirms the views already passed on the missing despatches and retreat of a party, although I was surprised to hear the late gallant veteran attribute the reason of Franklin leaving it empty as a proof that he did not go up Wellington Channel. Terminating our inquiry as to the origin of the traces found in 1850 at Beechey Island, our attention is drawn to those found near the junction of Jones' Sound with Wellington Channel. We speedily obtain our object by a reference to the despatch of Sir Edward Belcher, as it appeared in the *Morning Chronicle*, October 7th, 1854, wherein is given the following description of the traces found

by that officer:—" On the 20th of May, 1853
the open sea prevailed. The horizon was
streaked with open sailing ice, and all
communication cut off for sledges. The bluff,
distant sixteen miles, was clearly the turning
point into Jones' Channel; no land was visible
beyond it. Our progress was tantalizing and
attended with deep interest and excitement.
In the first place I discovered on the brow of a
mountain about 800 feet above the sea, what
appeared to be a recent and a very workman-
like structure of a dome (or rather a double cone
or ice-house), built of very heavy and tabular
slabs, which no single person could carry. It
consisted of about forty courses, eight feet in
diameter, and eight feet in depth when cleared,
but only five in height from the base of the
upper cone. As we opened it, most carefully
was every stone removed, every atom of moss or
earth scrutinized; the stones at the bottom also
taken up, but without a trace of any record, or
of having been used by any human being. It was
filled by drift snow, but did not in any respect
bear the appearance of having been built more
than a season. This was named Mount
Discovery. Our anxiety certainly was not
abated as we moved southerly, with every
appearance of a *cul de sac*, the channel opened
suddenly in a fresh direction, until at last,
having reached the bottom of a lake or bay, we
found that any further progress must be

confined to frozen streams or ravines, which connected with a series of great lakes leading into another sea.   Leaving the crew to pitch the tent, I ascended the mountain above us, and discovered that we were really not far from our old position last year on Cape Hogarth. My surprise, however, was suddenly checked by two structures in European form, and apparently graves.   Each was similarly constructed, and, like the dome, of large selected slabs, having at each end three separate stones laid as we would place head and feet stones; so thoroughly satisfied was I that there was no delusion, I desisted from disturbing a stone until it should be formally done by the party assembled.   The evening following we ascended the hill and removed the stones.   Not a trace of human beings.   If this had been a cache, and the carcase removed, I cannot understand why the stones should have been so carefully and systematically replaced.   Eventually, on digging to the hard quarry from which the cache had been clearly formed by art, we discovered a quantity of minute black dust, which, on examination by a powerful lens I found to be the chrysalis shells of minute flies, which might possibly have been generated by the remains of meal left here at a former date.   At various places we have found apparent marks, and had fancied that some of the explorers from the North Star (a ship lying at Beechey Island) had sought

Jones' Strait by this channel, but invariably every such mark had been placed where it could not serve the purpose of a geographical pile ; one in particular found by Mr. Grove on Pitch Mount, which he kept untouched until I examined it, was so methodically constructed of five stones that on the disturbance of any one the others would tumble ; and yet if Esquimaux had been concerned in its original structure how many years had it stood ? my own opinion is strongly in favour of a late visit, or within the last ten years." These then are the words of Sir Edward Belcher on the traces found in 1853, and it will be seen at a momentary glance they are full of interest ; because no European had visited that distant part before him. Experience has taught us that Esquimaux do not inhabit Jones' Sound or the shores of Wellington Channel, nor are they acquainted with the science of building by courses. Sir Edward was struck with the European form of the traces, and by their position was led to fancy that other explorers had previously sought Jones' Sound by the same channel he was in. They were not fixed to serve the purpose of a geographical pile, which with the replacing of the stones around the caches alone deceived him. That caches should be erected for that purpose far exceeds our expectations ; but that a building eight feet diameter and the same in height was erected on the brow of a mountain eight hundred feet above the sea for any other purpose than that of geography is not to be doubted. After solving a difficult problem by the lens, it appears surprising how the systematical placing of the stones could prove a masterpiece; he knew they were caches and that they had been emptied, therefore, a reconstruction was a true index to one great and important point, namely, those who emptied them expected to use them again; and as the retreating party of '49—50 consumed their contents they would leave them entire for their journey northward (after the remaining men,) should they find searching parties at Beechey Island, when they could again use them as before. Now as Franklin took the route north in '46 and paused to explore Jones' Sound it is not at all wonderful that others following on his track should find traces of him; and as he no doubt left provisions in caches near its junction with Wellington Channel, and a retreating party in '49 removed them, there can be as little wonder that Sir Edward Belcher in '53 should find them empty. A retreat could not have been made at any other period than in 1849—50, when the difficulties of Franklin's position were no longer doubtful, and when no ships were on search in Barrow Strait; had it been effected after that period the party must have been seen by some of the many searching expeditions as it passed southward. Sir Edward Belcher's despatch published in '54 had a wide circulation, but was treated with the same indifference as other features of the mystery, and though thousands must have been aware of the striking resemblance between the traces described in that despatch and those mentioned tion to the fact. The whalers' report appeared by a whaler crew in 1849 no one drew attenthus:—" In the season of '48 their ship (a Scotch whaler) entered Jones' Sound, and after running a hundred and fifty or two hundred miles up its southern shore, some of her crew landed and discovered a cairn, a fireplace, and footprints of Europeans; not having time to examine the cairn, as the captain finding he had mistaken this for Lancaster Sound, or a fog coming on, had them recalled, and being at a period when little or no anxiety was felt for the missing expedition, they attached no great importance to what they had seen; but when the public excitement arose after the return of Sir James Ross in November '49, they made a statement of the traces found in '48 while they were in Jones' Sound; adhering firmly to its truth they volunteered to pilot a ship back to the same place, and having that intention a few sailed in 1850 with Captain Penny's expedition, which made an attempt to enter that sound, but the heavy nature of the ice within it frustrated the attempt and compelled them to seek the indirect route by Wellington Channel. After their report had created great sensation in the public mind, Sir Edward Parry in February, '50, spoke of it as follows—" Considerable interest has lately been attached to Jones' Sound, from the fact of its having been recently navigated by at least one enterprising whaler, and found to be of great width, free from ice, with a swell from the westward, and having no land visible from the mast head in that direction, it seems more than probable, therefore, that it may be found to communicate with Wellington Channel; so that if Sir John Franklin's ships have been detained anywhere to the northward of Parry's Islands it would be by Jones' Sound that he would probably endeavour to effect his escape rather than by the less direct route of Barrow Strait."   The possibility of his attempting his escape through this fine opening, and the report of a cairn of stones seen by the whaler on a headland within it, seems to me to render it highly expedient to set this question at rest by a search in this direction; withholding all speculation, the whaler's report in seeing European footmarks or traces in '48 on the south shore of Jones' Sound is confirmed by the European form of the traces found by Sir Edward Belcher in the same direction, and at no great distance from the spot assigned to them by the whaler, therefore the last of three interesting facts being clearly established, we arrange them thus : the European form of the traces, the caches being found empty, and the discovery or exploration of Jones' Sound previous

to the visit of Sir Edward Belcher, and in reply
to the questions, who first discovered Jones'
Sound ? who left the caches, and who emptied
them ? a just and powerful explanation is found
in the course taken by Franklin in '46, and
by the retreat of his party in '49. On the 20th
of March 1848 Lady Franklin offered a reward
of £1000 to any whaler finding the lost
expedition in distress, and an additional sum of
£1000 to any ship which should at an early
period make extraordinary exertions for the
above object, and if required bring Sir John
Franklin and his party to England. These
rewards came out too late in the season of '48, as
by the 20th of March most of the ships had
sailed for the fishery; had a like sum been
offered to the whalers (throughout the seasons
of '47—48—49) to visit Cape Walker or Beechey
Island, their united efforts through successive
seasons would have been crowned with success;
but as it was the offer was not accepted because it
was indefinite : finding the lost expedition in
distress was an offer at random. The whalers
believed their search would have to be long and
far to find it, whereas, had the highly interesting
points of Cape Walker and Beechey Island been
particularly specified in the offer, they would then
have known the exact distance to go to reach
either of those places. Of course the value of
searching them within any of those seasons will
bear no measurement with a money standard.

Having followed the hero of the Polar sea from Beechey Island until the period of his mysterious retreat, and giving therein a clear delineation of the northern route, we continue (reserving to the conclusion of our subject the fate of Franklin and those left with the ships by the retreating party of '49). Meanwhile we should not be doing justice to this mysterious subject by considering the northern route alone, we ought not to be hasty in our conclusions, nor desirous of leading others away by a one sided view of our own, for it is by looking at the impossibilities of one route that we form our views on the probabilities of the other; the impossibilities of that by Cape Walker and Peel Sound far outweigh the probabilities of Wellington Channel. The world is now impressed with the belief that Franklin's ships have been wrecked in Victoria Strait or Peel Sound, this country above all others supports that view with a tenacity which nothing but ignorance can excuse, yet where is the evidence, either real or imaginary, for its foundation ; the dark paths of the mystery may be explored in vain for its origin, and were I not certain that further search for its volatile source would end in fatal disappointment, I would again make the attempt with pleasure, but experience teacheth wisdom, after one severe lesson we are taught to know better; let us, therefore, direct our thoughts to the route by Cape Walker and give every question relating to it due consideration.

We commence by presuming, as the world does, that Franklin in 1846, left Beechey Island with his ships, and stood away for Cape Walker, after reaching which he had a direct distance of two hundred and fifty miles southward to go to the north coast of King William's Land, the stated distance with Victoria Strait, making the north west passage, the great problem of centuries, and for which he was in search. From Cape Walker to the continent is just 380 miles. Allowing that contrary to his instructions, he passed that cape without leaving a despatch, he would then lead his ships south through Peel Sound. If we say they ran two hundred miles south of Cape Walker, here we behold them arrive on the scene of the supposed catastrophe at the close of the season of 1846, they would then be distant from King William's Land fifty miles, in the present unknown part of Peel Sound; passing the winter of 1846 here, and the spring of '47 arriving, his party would discover the north west passage by surveying the western shore of Victoria Strait, or by exploring the western coast of King William's Land.   Had no passage existed through Peel Sound, supposed by some to be a cul de sac, Franklin's attention would at once be fixed on pushing his ships north again to Barrow Strait, directing every effort in '47 towards that purpose.   But if a passage exists, as there is little reason to doubt, his first object after finding it would be to reach

the Great Fish River to communicate with Dr.
King, whose proposals to assist him in the search
were under consideration of the Admiralty at the
time he left England. He would, therefore, expect
Dr. King to descend that stream to assist him in the
summer of '47, were he not certain of meeting him
he knew that there was a great probability of his
coming that way. With this expectation, and
having but a short distance to travel, he would
send a party to meet him, and if necessary conduct him to the ships.   Why this was not done
in the seasons of '47 and '48, time must explain.
In the spring of '47 he must have found the
passage. His numerous parties would enable him
to explore both shores of Peel Sound and Victoria
Strait, with a large portion of the south coasts
of Victoria and Wollaston Lands in that season.
Unwishful to press this further, we grant that he
did not move his ships in '47, but patiently
waited the turn of '48, with the hope of effecting
their release. What detained him all this season,
his discoveries in a narrow channel three hundred miles long would be at an end?   Having
wintered in '48, what great feat had he to accomplish in '49, that he suffered this year also
to pass without an effort to escape, or an
attempt to seek the Esqimaux?   Was it still
the empty hope of rescuing his ships that he
sacrificed the lives of his men, or was it the
difficulty of pushing so large a body of men as
his ships' crews then consisted of down to the set-

tlements at one time?   In dividing them into
parties to make search in different directions for
relief, Franklin would have in view the
following routes, viz, by the Great Fish
River and on to Fort Resolution, — through
Ross Strait into Committee and Repulse Bays,
and southward to Fort Churchhill,—by Hood's
or the Coppermine Rivers to Fort Enterprise,—
a journey up Peel Sound to Cape Walker and
Barrow Strait,—and finally by pushing into
Prince Regent's Inlet, they could visit Port Leopold and Barrow Strait and thus intercept ships on
search. Here are five openings for communication or retreat.   And here are five questions
apparently beyond the powers of mankind to
answer.   We may be told those attempts have
been made and had failed, but how has every
attempt to escape by these five routes been alike
unsuccessful?   Here the absence of the expedition
is palpable to all.   Oh! say some, a catastrophe will account for all; but in what form
could a catastrophe so totally annihilate that
large and firm body of men as not to leave a trace
of them behind?   The mind cannot depict, nor the
pencil of imagination paint a calamity that
could in the suddenness of a moment sweep
those one hundred and thirty-five men from
the surface of the earth without leaving a mark
sufficient to show that they had once existed.
If the ships were in Peel Sound, and Franklin
found the attempt to reach the settlements im-
practicable, what deterred him from sending

a party to Cape Walker, and Bunny to place a despatch on both promontories stating the position of his ships, and the state of his crews. Cylinders containing this information could with ease have been put into Barrow Strait, and why was not another party sent up Prince Regent's Inlet to intercept ships on search going up the Strait? Fury Beach could be made the centre of that movement. Retreat back to the ships would not be difficult; despatches might have been left at Whaler Point; ships passing and finding them would know directly where to seek their position; yet forceable as all these may appear, they are weak when compared with the absence of Franklin's men from King William's Land and the continent until the spring of 1850, four years after they had left Beechey Island, Here is a fact that defies contradiction. This is the weapon that delivers the death stroke to the supposition of Franklin's ships being detained or wrecked in Peel Sound or Victoria Strait, and, when speaking of either passages, it carries us not only beyond imagination but to absolute conviction. I shall, therefore, continue to hold it as my unanswerable doctrine against the route by Peel Sound.

As the Esquimaux tribes hunt every season on the north of King William's Land, how singular it is that they did not see any of Franklin's parties (whose ships were so near) before the spring of 1850, and no less marvellous does it appear, that those parties did not visit that coast in search of the passage and of Esquimaux. Was Franklin restrained four years within fifty miles of that coast without a chance of once reaching it? Are we to believe that with his ships and crews, he lay from the season of '46 until that of '50, within easy reach of Esquimaux, within fifty miles of the object of his search, and still did not accomplish it? Can we for a moment entertain the monstrous improbability that he remained in a useless position until the health and strength of his crews were exhausted, until his provisions were gone, and that when death appeared before him in the spring of 1850 he despatched a starving party towards the continent, and gave it so little food that they were compelled to purchase a seal from the natives on the north coast of King William's Land, a distance of fifty miles from the ships? Had they been in Peel Sound would Dr. Rae in 1851 have searched the whole south coast of Victoria Land without finding a mark of their numerous parties? would he have pushed up Victoria Strait, the scene of the supposed catastrophe itself, without finding trace? It is these and such as these that form the impossibilities by Cape Walker and Peel Sound; they are the facts as clear as noon-day and as simple as they are clear. We may compare Franklin's position between the seasons of '46—'50 to that of Sir John Ross in those from '29 to '33, as in geogra-

phy they would be nearly similar.   Sir John Ross
had one ship and twenty-eight men, and that
ship was not fitted up with anything like the
scientific perfections that the missing ships were,
nor had he half the number of experienced
officers as had Franklin, yet let us speak of the
labours of those few men.   They fixed their
winter quarters in Felix Harbour September 1829,
and on January 9th, 1830, received a visit from
a large tribe of Esquimaux.   In May '30 they
explored the north coast of King William's Land,
completing a journey altogether of 400 miles ;
in the following season they crossed Boothia and
discovered the magnetic pole.   They made
journeys around lakes and inlets, surveying a
considerable extent of coast, receiving while travelling valuable assistance from the Esquimaux ;
and when in the spring of '32 a retreat became
necessary, they made first to Fury Beach, a distance by the coast lineof at least 200 miles, from
that point to Barrow Strait, where they remained full three weeks struggling for a passage
eastward.   Being foiled in that attempt they ran
back to Fury Beach, and in the season of '33
again ascended Prince Regent's Inlet, where, after
pushing eastward through Barrow Strait to Navy
Board Inlet they were found by a whaler.   The
single boat journeys of Ross extended from the
north coast of King William's Land to the
entrance of Navy Board Inlet, a distance
of seven or eight hundred miles.   His party

twice crossed Boothia, and traversed the shores
of Prince Regent's Inlet thrice in attempting to
escape, and still he was saved. Whereas it is
affirmed that between M. Bellot's position in
1852 on the western shore of Peel Sound and
the north coast of King William's Land, a distance
of one hundred and fifteen miles, is concealed
the whole mystery of the Franklin expedition.
Franklin with two ships and one hundred and
thirty-five men must be five years absent, within
a space of one hundred and fifteen miles, and
have nothing to show for his labours but the
loss of his ships and crews in a manner so complete as to resist all detection. By Dr. Rae's
discoveries on the shores of Victoria Strait in '51
it was proved that Franklin had not found the
passage in that direction ; and by the Esquimaux
narrative his party did not reach the north coast
of King William's Land, or complete the survey
of one hundred and fifteen miles until four years
had passed from leaving Beechey Island. Did
this trifle master the whole science and experience of that famous expedition ? Is this what it
has been twelve years absent upon ? The more
we think of this subject the greater appears the
public deception. It is difficult to close on the
route by Peel Sound without alluding to the
search already made upon its shores and the
open water known to exist in Victoria Strait.
In May 1849 Sir James Ross led his party from
Port Leopold, and traced the coast of north

Somerset as far west as Cape Bunny, after
which he turned to the southward and followed
its western coast to a position in latitude 72—38
north, or a distance of one hundred and forty
miles south of that cape. Arrived at his fur-
thest point he thus describes the scene before
him. "The state of the atmosphere being
peculiarly favourable for the distinctness of vision,
land of any great elevation might have been seen
at a distance of one hundred miles, the highest
cape of the coast was not more than fifty miles
distant, bearing nearly due south." This obser-
vation leaves no doubt whatever as to Peel Sound
being a channel; Ross must have all but sighted
the northern coast of King William's Land, as it
was within one hundred and forty miles of his
position. He then returned to his ships without
a mark or trace of the lost expedition, and in
May 1851 Commander Osborne visited Cape
Walker and carried his explorations down the
western shore of Peel Sound to a situation ninety
miles south of that cape, returning also without
a trace. In 1852 M. Bellot traversed both
shores of Peel Sound, carrying his survey on its
western to a distance of one hundred and fifty
miles south of Cape Walker, and on that of its
eastern to nearly the same distance. His search,
like the rest, proved unsuccessful. In the season of 1851 Dr. Rae crossed from the continent
of America north to Victoria Land, and after
following sixteen degrees of longitude from west

to east pushed his party up Victoria Strait to a position in latitude 70—20 north, longitude 101 west, or within one hundred miles of that attained by M. Bellot on the western shore of Peel Sound; he likewise retraced his steps without anything to reward his search. We may extend the above search by adding the explorations of Dr. Rae in '53—'54 on the western coast of Boothia, when he traced that coast from Castor and Pollux River northward to Cape Porter. Here then we behold an extent of search truly astonishing, and here is a search all conducted on foot. There can be no mistake of lands, of cairns, or traces, as there might if ships had been engaged. And as this is certain evidence, we cannot but dwell on the reflection that in all that long and barren search not a mark or trace was found sufficient to show how those lands had ever been trodden by the foot of man. It may be said of its results, had one individual perished in attempting the passage through Peel Sound, less marks of him could not have been found than there have been of the missing navigators.

Concerning the open water known to exist in the passage between Cape Walker and the continent, it is generally found turning the south-east point of Victoria Land, and connecting itself with the waters of the great bay which Messrs. Dease and Simpson navigated with their boats in 1839. Upon examination of a chart of those regions, we must expect to find open water in Victoria Strait, and in the large space to the south-west, as it is the only part that has freedom. Peel Sound is seldom, if ever, disturbed, because King William's Land acts as a shield against the passage of the ice southward. Victoria Strait seems too narrow to admit of the large bodies of ice in Peel Sound passing through it into the great bay; nor is there a current possessed of sufficient strength to force it through. If, therefore, open water exists annually in this strait, the difficulties Franklin would have to encounter in passing to the southward would be small indeed. Had he pushed through Peel Sound in '46, his escape by Victoria Sound would become an easy task; surprising, indeed, it would be if he could pass through the ice-locked portion of Peel Sound, with all its attending difficulties, into that strait in one season, and that the open water therein should not only detain him four years, but eventually prove his ruin.

From the position of the lands around Peel Sound, and in the absence of a strong current, the ice to be found within it is not berg or packed ice, but heavy floes or hummocky field ice, formed therein through successive seasons. Its undisturbed nature entitles it to the name of one of the most impenetrable channels in the Arctic regions. As the main features of both routes have now been clearly brought to notice it is needless to go further into detail regarding them ; and without indulging in the belief that both have been dealt with as they ought— we press forward to consider the result of some of the most important searching expeditions. In June, 1848, Sir James Ross, with two ships proceeded in search of Franklin; commencing his search in Pond's Bay, he followed it up to Port Leopold, which he entered September 11th, 1848, and here he passed the winter, little, if anything, further being done by him that season. Were it not for a timely declaration made by Sir John Ross, we could not have learned why Sir James Ross paid no heed to the most interesting points in the line of search, namely, Cape Walker and Beechey Island ; had a few men been sent to that Cape immediately after reaching Port Leopold, they would have learnt by no despatch being left there, that Franklin had not pursued the south-west course, having erected a cairn recording the position of their ships, they could have then returned to Port Leopold. This must have produced two effects—first, it would alter the line of search from south to north, while the cairn on Cape Walker would show to any retreating party the presence of a relief expedition. Had the season of '48 been too far advanced to admit of such a step, why was it shamelessly neglected in 1849. The erection of

a cairn on Cape Walker in either seasons must
have saved the lives of at least the retreating
party, if not the whole expedition.   That party
passing early in the season of 1850, would have
seen the cairn, and have learnt by the despatch
where to find assistance.   The parties under
Sir James Ross searched the south shore of
Barrow Strait as far west as Cape Bunny,
they visited Fury Beach, and both shores of
Prince Regent's Inlet, but without finding a trace
of the missing expedition.   If the discovery of
the north west passage had not been the object
of his intentions, why did he follow the western
coast of North Somerset, one hundred and forty
miles south of Cape Bunny instead of making
direct for Cape Walker?   What else but the
passage induced him to attach more importance
to a barren journey of one hundred and forty
miles, than to that cape distant but forty miles ?
His intention of finding the passage and neglecting Franklin is observed throughout his search
in a light too painful to be passed unnoticed.
The work was well done by his parties, but it
was quite in the wrong direction, and the entire
absence of marks or traces surely must have
told him so.   It will scarcely receive credence
that the expedition of '48 lay in sight of and
within eighty miles of Beechey Island for twelve
months, without making one effort to reach
either it or Cape Walker.   By the subtle means
adopted the first winter quarters of Franklin at

that island remained undiscovered until the autumn of '50, and through treachery Cape Walker lay unvisited until the spring of '51, and what was the result of this culpable conduct? why, that the retreating party had passed unobserved. Had that expedition been properly conducted, Franklin's winter quarters at Beechey Island and the now missing despatches would have been found in '49, while, had another despatch and a supply of provisions been left close by, they would have afforded the means of placing the party in comparative security. How simply now appears the remedy that could have arrested those few fatal months, and instead of carrying those brave men to destruction, have led them to where relief was to be found. It is painful in the extreme to reflect on the proceedings of the expedition of '48, especially as its barren effects arose from self-aggrandizement; with amazement we beheld its sudden termination, and when the mind strikes into the depths of the mystery it recoils, stricken and appalled at the consequences which have followed its disastrous results. Time must and will reveal it; when the dark curtain which now covers the melancholy fate of our countrymen is but once lifted, these disclosures will tell home with painful effect.

In the narrative of Sir John Ross, published in 1855, p. 32, he is found thus addressing Lord Auckland (first Lord of the Admiralty) on the eve

E

of the departure of Sir James Ross in 1848.
" He can have no intention of searching for Sir
John Franklin : his object is the passage by surveying the western coast of North Somerset."
It might be imagined this singular address arose
from a feeling we ought to pass in silence,
but as the search made by Sir James faithfully
confirmed its truth, it becomes a subject worthy
of our attention.   Universal pity will ever plead
for the man who, after a life of usefulness to
his country, hazards all for the knowledge of
mankind, but that man who hazards all the
honours acquired during an active life, and will
make every sacrifice for the mere gratification of
a selfish purpose must ever be held in detesta-
tion.   Such an audacious parade of selfishness
should have been upheld to receive from the world
that chastisement which was its due ; never did a
base action better merit that well known term—
the vilest of the vile ; it then was a matter of total
indifference to Sir James Ross where Franklin
had gone, or under what privations his gallant
companions were suffering.   In due time the
public will find double cause to bitterly denounce
the inhuman motives that led to the disasters of
the expedition of 1848, it will then learn that a
more heartless and deliberate instance of wanton
sacrifice, shrouded by selfishness and hypocrisy,
never stained the annals of this country.   Its
author should reflect on the past even though

he possess but the slightest shade of conscience, for he smothered the soul-stirring cries of his ill fated countrymen, he consigned to eternal imprisonment, woe, and oblivion the lives of those who for the benefit of science suffered as martyrs, and who truly deserved a nobler fate. It was to meet this reward that noble band of gallant Englishmen struggled on against famine, perils, and misfortunes, cherishing again and again, as in vain and in vain, some fond but forlorn hope of succour; it was this treatment which forced them to lay down their weary lives on a barren land, to which the human foot was a stranger, and where lie their unburied remains. Their sufferings and the whole mystery of their fate might be undiscovered for years, for ages, or perhaps for ever. It was to such men as these they willingly resigned the sweets of liberty and all that was dear to them in this world; into the hands of these individuals they entrusted their valuable lives. Had Franklin and his companions laid down their bones on a bleak Arctic waste as a repast for the wild and ferocious bears of the north, or have sought in the desolate wilderness of their woes for a solitary living object upon which to fix their affection, they would have had it returned with tenfold more effect than by some of their own selfish and disgraceful countrymen. The results of all the searching expeditions that have been engaged since the return of Sir James Ross in 1849, are as nothing when compared with the results of his expedition, and although we cannot but conclude on its proceedings, still they remain the centre upon which works the mystery.

CHAPTER II.

In the spring of '50, Captain Austin, Sir John Ross, and Captain Penny, left England for Barrow Strait, and in the month of August arrived at Beechey Island. They discovered Franklin's winter quarters and the traces hitherto spoken of. On Captain Penny's parties exploring Wellington Channel and finding open water in and around its northern entrance, Penny exclaimed, ' through this channel Franklin has gone in clear water,' soliciting at the same time the loan of a steamer to push through it, but as every one knows without success. On Beechey Island Penny's men found three graves left by Franklin, the date of the latest death being April 3rd, 1846. On Cape Spencer in Wellington Channel they found a look out or watch tent, which doubtless had been pitched on that promontory to watch the movements of the ice in that channel, previous to the departure of Franklin in 1846, This trace is interesting as regards the course taken by Franklin from Beechey Island, it clearly proving that he expected open water in Wellington Channel, and was attentively watching for an opening to proceed northward. A trace found on a hill near the graves likewise deserves our notice, as it strongly indicates the caution used by him while at Beechey Island : this was a hand board nailed to a boarding pike eight feet long, with the hand painted black.

When it was brought to England near the close of 1851, the general opinion was, that it had formed one of many, fixed to direct parties back to the ships ; a view which does not appear very intelligible, as the ships lying in a cove or small bay, their crews must have known exactly where to seek them ; a conclusion more to the purpose is, that the black hand was set up as an emblem of death, near the graves, to direct searching parties to them. As lying in the valley beneath, Franklin would know that without some mark as a guide, searching parties might not find them. He therefore had set it up on the hill close by for that object; it was found broken and lying on its face, the back of the board was perforated with swan shot, a circumstance which accounts for its being found as above. Here the English expeditions were joined by an American one (under Com. Dr. Haven,) which in Barrow Strait was caught with the ice and carried eastward through Lancaster Sound in the same manner as was Sir James Ross in 1849, leaving our expeditions to continue the search. The season of '51 having arrived, Sir John Ross and Captain Austin directed their parties towards Melville Island. An extensive coastline was explored, but no trace found of the missing ships. Captains Austin and Penny made an attempt to reach Cape Walker with their ships, and though the former was aided by steam it was impossible to overcome the obstacles presented by the ice in that direction. That Cape was at length visited in '51 by Commander Osborne's party, thus leaving us to place on record a flagrant instance of gross injustice to the lost heroes, for Franklin being instructed to go first to Cape Walker, would necessarily expect that it would be the first place visited by searching parties. Did England send those daring seamen on such a perilous mission with three years' provisions only, and suffer them to be absent six long years without once causing to be searched the first place which they were ordered to visit? Yes, such was the fact, and however strange it may appear, is nevertheless true. There had they been throughout that period exploring distant lands for the glory of their country, undergoing trials and sufferings which no pen can describe, and England, dear England, had not searched Cape Walker, the very place to which the missing expedition was directed first to proceed. It is a very deep reflection that had Franklin sent a party from Beechey Island in '46 to place a despatch on that cape (with the belief that it would soon be found,) we must have beheld the consequences of neglect in the loss of the expedition, whereas had he gone south through Peel Sound in '46 and had left a despatch on Cape Walker, or after being three years fixed in that sound had sent up to that cape expressing in another despatch the alarming nature of his position, it would have been found too late to save a living being. This nation would then have been confounded by its own cold and careless actions ; it may derive a little satisfaction in finding no despatch on Cape Walker in '51, yet the neglect in not searching it before that period was no less cruel than it is unpardonable. Parties from the expedition of '50 traced the shores of Melville and Peel Sound, the south coast of Parry's Islands, and the shores of Lancaster Sound, but beyond the traces found in the vicinity of Beechey Island, nothing important rewarded their search. They remained in Barrow Strait until August '51, and then returned home, leaving in Wellington Channel fifteen miles of ice. Captain Penny's opinion afterwards on this ice was, that it probably cleared out a few days after they left it ; he had seen greater changes in forty-eight hours. No sooner had they returned than two reports at once attracted public attention, a ridiculous story of Franklın's sbips having been burnt and their crews murdered near Cape Duddley Diggs (in Baffin's Bay), and a vague report made by the captain of a merchant vessel who, while crossing the banks of Newfoundland in April 1850 saw two ships in some heavy field ice. Upon the first it would be a waste of time to dwell, and Captain Coward's report merely connects the missing expedition by a slight comparison between the time he saw the ships and the time Franklin's party was seen approaching King William's Land.

Let us now glance at the opinions of several eminent Arctic navigators on the position of the missing ships.

In February 1847, Sir John Ross believed them to be frozen up somewhere to the westward of Melville Island.

A dread hung over Sir John Barrow (the founder of the expedition), when in July '47, he says, the only chance of bringing them upon the American coast, is the possibility of some obstruction having tempted them to explore an immense inlet on the northern shore of Barrow Strait short of Melville Island called Wellington Channel, which Parry felt an inclination to explore, and more than one of the present party betrayed to me a similar inclination, which I discouraged, no one venturing to conjecture even to what extent it might go, or into what difficulties it might lead

Three opinions are found given by Captain
Beechey, December 1st, 1849. I entirely agree
with Sir Francis Beaufort and Sir Edward Parry,
that the expedition is probably hampered among
the ice somewhere to the south westward of
Melville Island.

Time having revealed to Sir Edward Parry
the inconsistency of that view, in 1852 he
declared his belief that Franklin had gone so
far up Wellington Channel in the favourable
season of 1846 as to be unable to return.

February 7th, 1850, Sir John Richardson
was of opinion that Franklin had pushed on to
Cape Walker without stopping, and in attempting
to penetrate to the south-west, he became involved
in the drift ice which at that time was supposed
to exist, and was carried in that direction towards
Coronation Gulf. At the same period, Dr.
McCormic speaks thus :—" Wellington Channel
of all the probable openings into the Polar Sea
possesses the highest degree of interest, and the
exploration of it is of such paramount importance
that I should have comprised it within my plan
of search, had not the Enterprise and Investigator,
(ships of Sir James Ross in '48), had orders to
examine this inlet and Cape Walker." After
tendering his services he concludes in these
terms, " I see no reason for changing the opinion
I entertained last spring,('49) subsequent events
have only tended to confirm them. I then believed,
and I do so still, after a long and mature consideration of the subject, that Sir John Franklin's

ships have been arrested in a high latitude, and beset in the heavy Polar ice northward of Parry's Islands." This appears to me to be the only view of the case that can in any way account for the entire absence of all tidings of them throughout so protracted a period of time, unless all have perished by some sudden and over-whelming catastrophe. Isolated as their position would be under such circumstances, any attempt to reach the continent of America at such a distance would be hopeless in the extreme, and the mere chance of any party from the ships reaching the top of Baffin's Bay at the very moment of a whaler's brief and uncertain visit would be attended with by far too great a risk to justify the attempt, for failure would ensure inevitable destruction to the whole party, there-fore, their only alternative would be, to keep together in their ships should no disaster have happened to them, and by husbanding their re-maining resources, eke them out with whatever wild animals may come within their reach.

The decision of Captain Austin is seen by his despatch dated August 12th, '51, wherein he says, " I have arrived at the conclusion that the expedi-tion under Sir John Franklin did not prosecute the object of its mission to the southward and westward of Wellington Channel, and having considered the search of that channel by the expedition under Captain Penny, I do not feel authorised to prosecute (even if practicable) a

further search in those directions." Out of this
arose the unwarrantable view that Franklin,
unable to accomplish his object in '45—'46, had
turned his ships homeward and was lost while
on his return.

Few just men attached any importance to that
view, and as it more seriously affected his
character it will meet a refutation when we speak
of that subject.   Opinions were given by many
other celebrated Arctic voyagers, but as it is
needless to bring them all to notice, we conclude
by rehearsing the opinions of Dr. King in 1848,
which became doubly interesting in 1854, when
the Esquimaux narrative was published by Dr.
Rae. The views of Dr. King were, that Franklin
was able so far to obey his orders as to push
his ships between Melville Island and Banks'
Land ; assuming therefore that he has been arrested between those lands, where Sir Edward Parry
was arrested by difficulties which he considered in-
surmountable, and he has followed the advice of
that gallant officer, and made for the continuity
of America, he will have turned the prows of
his vessels south and west according as Banks'
Land tends for Victoria and Wollaston Lands.
It is here, therefore, that we may expect to find
the expedition wrecked ; whence they will make
in their boats for the western land of North
Somerset, if that land be not too far distant.
The position I assign to the expedition is that
coast midway between the settlements of the

Hudson's Bay Company on the Mackenzie River
and the fishing ground of the whalers in Pond's
Bay. They would make that coast for the
double purpose of reaching Barrow Strait in
search of whalers, as Sir John Ross did success-
fully, and the great Fish River in search of
Esquimaux for provisions or for letter conveyance
to the copper Indians with whom the Esquimaux
are now on friendly terms

Dr. King nobly volunteered to conduct
an expedition overland down the Great Fish
River as early as 1847, and as late as 1856
in search of Franklin; but instead of a
favourable reception, he met from the Admiralty a fierce opposition. When that
board in '47—'48 believed, as it really did, that
Franklin was able to obey the first part of his
instructions by passing south-west of Cape
Walker, in what direction did it hope to prosecute
a successful search with land parties than by
descending the Great Fish River and proceeding
north-west, or by going down the Coppermine River and striking off north-east. Within
that period the justice of Dr. King's views must
have appeared plain to the Admiralty or to the
Arctic council, but originating with an independent yet highly distinguished Polar traveller,
they were opposed by those who, unfortunately,
had the fatal power to display a spirit of
rejection.

When their Lordships felt convinced that

Franklin had passed Cape Walker no time should have been lost in ascertaining the fact. Then if they felt a pleasure in neglecting this important place, they should have relinquished the search to others, who would have taken as great delight in its prosecution. Had Dr. King been allowed to descend the Great Fish River, as he proposed in '50, he would probably have saved the lives of the retreating party : he required the pompous title of R. N. to his name—because it was unattached Franklin must suffer. We are not surprised that great difference of opinion should exist concerning his mysterious fate, but that such difference of opinion should lead to the sacrifice of one hundred and thirty-five fellow creatures, says but little for the times in which we live. How many interesting events would be hushed up, and important subjects entirely neglected if the power of control was lodged in the hands of a few. If one man claims the right of forming his own opinions, another claims the power of rejecting them. Man may reduce to slavery his fellow man. The elevated position of one in this life may give him power to cut the small thread that confines the existence of another to this world; but to the Supreme Being alone belongs the right to control the mind. Too often men holding responsible situations in the government of a country are so self-conceited that they will not receive advice from others, though they possess greater abilities, and are independent of them. Nor is it uncommon for them to look on the working classes as beings unfit to exist in the same atmosphere with themselves. Dr. King, as an experienced voyager, proposed to the Lords of the Admiralty a plan of search for Franklin, and because he maintained his opinions was considered presumptuous. Did the very high positions of their Lordships give them power to see through the mystery? Was great wealth and a great name to accomplish all? In so thinking they purchased a frail imagination by a dreadful sacrifice.

With due order in our progress we arrive at the Esquimaux narrative and traces found in 1848 by Dr. Rae, the report attending the discovery of which is thus briefly told by that enterprising traveller.—"During my journey over the ice and snows this spring, with the view of completing the survey of the west coast of Boothia, I met with Esquimaux in Pelly Bay, from one of whom I learnt that a party of white men had perished from want of food some distance to the westward, and not far beyond a large river containing many falls and rapids. Subsequently further particulars were received, and a number of articles purchased, which places the fate of a portion, if not all of the then survivors of Sir John Franklin's long lost party, beyond a doubt—a fate as terrible as the imagination can conceive."

The substance of the information obtained at various times and from various sources, was as follows :—" In the spring, four winters past, —spring of '50—a party of white men, amounting to about forty, were seen travelling southward over the ice and dragging a boat with them, by some Esquimaux, who were killing seals near the north coast of King William's Land which is a large island. None of the party could speak the Esquimaux language intelligibly, but by signs the natives were made to understand that their ship or ships had been crushed in the ice, and that they were now going where they expected to find deer to shoot. From the appearance of the men, all of whom, except one officer, looked thin, they were then supposed to be getting short of provisions, and they purchased a small seal from the° natives. At a later date the same season, but previous to the breaking up of the ice, the bodies of some thirty persons were discovered on the conti- nent, and five on an island near it, about a long day's journey to the north-west of a large stream, (which can be no other than the Great Fish River,) some of the bodies had been buried, somewhere in a tent or tents, others under the boat, which had been turned up to form a shelter, and several lay scattered about in different directions. Of those found on the island, one was supposed to have been an officer, as he had a telescope strapped over his shoulder, and his double-barrelled gun lay beneath him. From the mutilated state of many of the corpses, and the contents of the kettles, it is evident that our wretched countrymen had been driven to the last resource, cannibalism, as a means of prolonging existence. There must have been a number of watches, compasses, telescopes, guns, several double-barrelled, &c., all of which appear · to have been broken up, as I saw pieces of these different articles with the Esquimaux, and together with some silver spoons and forks, purchased as many as I could get. None of the Esquimaux with whom I conversed had seen the whites, nor had they ever been at the place where the bodies were found, but had their information from those who had been there and who had seen the party when travelling.

The relics found by Dr. Rae consisted of silver spoons and forks, Franklin's Guelphic badge or star, a piece of plate marked " Sir John Franklin, K. C. H.," the remains of a boat compass, pieces of hatbands, guns, watches, knives, buttons, and clothing, together with part of a book called the " Student's Manual." Let us pay no attention to hearsay evidence, but give this report an impartial consideration.

They say first that the white men purchased a seal, though we are not told what they gave for it, and by the contents of their kettles the

F

party had resorted to cannibalism, which is a very grave charge, but is reasonably maintained, not so much by the mutilated state of the bodies, as by the absence of five men after the party had been several months in a state of starvation. On the other hand, five may have died on the journey from the north coast of King William's Land to the continent, or the Esquimaux may not have seen forty men on that coast as first represented. Taking into view the difficulties of that journey and their feeble condition, it is possible that five may have died therein. But the chance of those five being still alive among the Esquimaux is almost too faint to sustain hope. If they are, it is surprising they could not reach the settlements, or at least send intelligence of their position before this protracted period There is an extraordinary simplicity and truthful bearing in the Esquimaux statement of seeing forty men straitened for provisions, to such an extent as to compel them to purchase a seal, (no doubt for food), near the north coast of King William's Land, and in finding a few months afterwards on the continent but thirty-five bodies and the party resorting to cannibalism: the purchasing of a seal accords faithfully with their starving appearance, and if their journey proved unsuccessful in shooting or fishing after having seen the Esquimaux, a few weeks, not months, would reduce them to that condition represented by those tribes. Had they said there were forty white men when first seen and found forty dead, the falsehood of resorting to cannibalism would be instantly detected; they based their report on the mutilated state of the bodies and the contents of their kettles, and not from the absence of five bodies, which goes far to prove the truth of their statements. Being ignorant of the real evidence, and as we cannot fully rely on the Esquimaux statements, we can, however, test their truth by circumstances.

That the party perished a long day's journey to the north west of a large stream seems nearly correct, but as there is doubtless a mistake in the interpretation of that position, we defer the subject until we notice the voyage of Mr. Anderson in '55 down the Great Fish River. The Esquimaux seen by Dr. Rae, say they did not see the white men while living, nor had they been to the place where their bodies were found, but received their information from those who had been there. In this they represent a falsehood, for if they had seen the white men but a few days previous to meeting Dr. Rae, they could not have given a more minute description of the melancholy scene. In that statement we are told of their starving appearance when first seen; that they were going to the hunting grounds to shoot deer; their ships had been crushed in the ice; their getting short of provisions, their purchasing a seal; and of finding afterwards but thirty-five bodies; the contents of the kettles; the exact position of an officer with a

telescope strapped on his shoulders and a gun
beneath him ; that five bodies were found on an
island — doubtless an advance party ; the
boat turned up to form a shelter; the time
accurately fixed between the spring when first
seen and the breaking up of the ice when found
dead ; all of which statements are so firmly allied
with reason, as to leave but little doubt as to their
truth. Had the story been communicated through
other tribes to those seen by Dr. Rae, would
they have been able to spin so fine a thread as
this ? Could they have given every particular of
the retreating party while living, and every con-
ceivable position of their bodies after their death ?
There must have been a vivid impression left on
their minds, and such an impression as could not
be left by the language of others. It is clearly evident that they had been eye witnesses of the scene
itself, or they could not have produced such in-
stantaneous and correct colourings. The pro-
pensity of the Esquimaux tribes for pilfering and
falsehood is too well known for us to put trust
in all they say, but like the statement of a criminal
when it is borne out by circumstances and by reason, we are bound to believe in its truth. Is it at all
likely that another tribe would deliver to the one
seen by Dr. Rae, the articles of ornament enume-
rated by him and upon which they set so great a
value ? But granting that they heard such a story
from others, would they not on hearing it immediately make off to the scene of plunder ? It is but

reasonable to suppose that those who arrived first
at the scene of death would select those articles
most attractive to the eye, and leave the weighty
or unsightly ones to a future period. Among the
traces found by Dr. Rae we have the star of
Franklin, pieces of plate, hatbands, watches, buttons, clothing, all of them relics so closely connected with the remains of our countrymen, that we
are perfectly convinced that those Esquimaux
who possessed them not only saw them while
living but were first on the desolate scene of
plunder after they were dead. It is a very interesting fact, that in the list of relics there are no
traces connecting them with the missing ships,
and a no less remarkable circumstance, that in
that list there is a piece of plate belonging to
nearly every officer in the lost expedition, and
but one piece. Why this clear distinction?
Had we required the crests or initials of every
officer missing, it would have been difficult to
get a better selection than those inscribed on
the plate found by Dr. Rae. Both Franklin and
Crozier had much plate with them, yet singular
it is that but one piece was found belonging to
either, and that conspicuously marked with their
initials and crests. Now there being but one
piece of plate belonging to each of those officers
they may have sent it with the retreating party to
barter with the Esquimaux for provision or as tokens of their affection for home. Had they been
sent to exchange for provisions, it shows

that the party was prepared against any difficulty which might arise in its journey, and able to purchase therewith succour from the Esquimaux ; at the same time it is clear that nothing but a long distance from the continent could have induced Franklin to send his star and plate for that object.   Having sent them to barter for provisions, and knowing they would be conspicuously worn by the Esquimaux and seen by searching parties, we imagine he would have marked thereon the latitude and longitude with the date of his position, so that any party finding them would seek his position and render him assistance.

The discovery of Franklin's star leads to the conviction that having parted with his honours, the circumstances under which he did so were extraordinary ; in this there is something intensely interesting and sublime, as why should he part with his star, the reward of his sufferings, the bright symbol of the glories for which he had struggled through life? He has bid it adieu with the thoughts of the grave, or with the sad reflection of being consigned to all the horrors of a Polar dungeon.   Being unable to accomplish the passage at the period when the retreating party left him, his isolated position so far north and at such a distance from the civilized world, might cause him to doubt whether he would ever again behold the shores of his own native land.

On the Esquimaux Dr. Rae saw the remains
of many watches. What necessity was there
for the white men to have so many watches?
They did not require the use of them all to keep
time when they had chronometers for that purpose. Unable to see their utility it is probable
they were sent with the star and plate that was
marked as tokens of remembrance from the lost
navigators to their families or friends, who would
at once recognize in them every tie of earthly
sympathy. Dr. Rae's arrival in '54 created a
great sensation ; the narrative and traces, when
made known were looked upon by some as the
last tidings that could be obtained of the missing expedition. The story was hastily handled
by the press, and the public assured itself nothing
more was to be done but to visit Point Ogle or
Montreal Island, and there unveil the whole
mystery.

The clamour of that time forms a strong
contrast to the silence that ensued in 1855, when
the results of Mr. Anderson's voyage down
the Great Fish River became known, the
vaunted confidence at first displayed baffles all
description, and without making a source of
pleasure of a subject that should be one of
sorrow, we proceed in the following chapter to
arrange the results of the last named undertaking.

CHAPTER III.

The expedition under Mr. Anderson left Fort
Resolution on Great Slave Lake, June 20th,
1355, and descending the Great Fish River,
found near its mouth traces enough to confirm
the leading feature of the Esquimaux narrative
given to Dr. Rae, namely, that a party from the
missing ships had suffered in the direction indicated.   The traces found, consisted of kettles and
tent poles, pieces of oars, part of a blue flag, a piece
of wood supposed to be the remains of a boat
marked Terror, another piece of wood said to
be part of a snow shoe, upon which was cut Mr.
Stanley (surgeon of the Erebus), a shovel, and chi-
sels, pieces of instruments, a letter nip, a bar of un-
wrought iron three feet long, one and a half inch
broad, and a quarter of an inch thick, together
with a few other articles comprised the whole;
they were found on Montreal Island, and on the
Esquimaux residing near the entrance of the
Great Fish River no trace was found at Point

Ogle nor on the north-east coast of Adelaide Peninsula; not even a scrap of paper could be discovered, and though a minute search was made not a vestige of the remains of the retreating party was found. The relics described appear to have been carried some distance by the Esquimaux, as from their peculiar nature it is evident that Franklin's party neither reached Point Ogle nor Montreal Island. On a strict examination we fail to find the least trace connecting their remains with either places. The difference between those found by Dr. Rae and the traces found by Mr. Anderson is too wide to escape notice. The former relics all connect the remains of the lost party, there being in the list not only knives, plate, and watches, but also hatbands, buttons, and remains of clothing, which undoubtedly must have been taken from their bodies, whereas we behold the entire absence of such articles in those found by Mr. Anderson. All he discovered were traces of a boat; there can be no doubt as to their having belonged to Franklin's men, but the absence of papers and bodies, as of traces connecting them with the Great Fish River, is a never failing proof that they have not been detained nor have they perished on its shores. An Esquimaux woman informed Mr. Anderson that when her tribe arrived only one white man was living, and he it was too late to save. If her statement be true they must have been plundered long before the last man ceased to exist ; the star, the plate, and watches, with the other valuables had gone before this tribe arrived, otherwise they would have selected those things before tent poles, oars, kettles, and such like cumbersome articles. That forty Englishmen suffered themselves to be plundered of everything so long as one of them could stand is not to be credited. When Franklin with sixteen men beat off nearly three hundred Esquimaux in July 1826 at the entrance of the Mackenzie River, it may well be believed that he was not with the forty in 1850. The Esquimaux narrative says their remains were found at a long day's journey to the north-west of a large stream, said to be the Great Fish River ; the position was interpreted as Point Ogle and Montreal Island, and if the stream spoken of is that river those places are not a long day's journey to the north-west of it as they are within that stream. When hearing of a ship- wreck at a point a long day's journey north of the Thames, we naturally begin our calculation from its northern boundary. The width of the Great Fish River has been taken for the long day's journey instead of that distance from its western entrance. To the north-west of any object of course means in that direction from it. Dr. Rae was further informed that the white men perished from want, some distance to the westward, and not far beyond a large river, thus clearly showing the position to be without and

not within the stream.   In directing our eyes to
a chart to follow the retreating party on its
journey southward from the north coast of King
William's Land, we behold them pushing down
its western coast towards the continent, which
to reach would compel them to cross Simpson
Strait, but if desirous of making direct towards
the Great Fish River they would continue on the
south coast of King William's Land, attempting
their object by travelling eastward through
Simpson Strait until they arrived off the mouth
of that stream.

The first portion of the continent seen on
their route would be the north-west coast of
Adelaide Peninsula.   Now the question is which
course was most practicable to them at that time ;
to cross Simpson Strait on to Adelaide Peninsula,
or to continue eastward and reach the entrance of
the Great Fish River.   Had they attempted the
former, the position I assign to their remains is the
north-west coast of that peninsula, and as there
is a large island off that coast this may be the
spot indicated by the Esquimaux narrative ; the
position named by those tribes may also be
applied to the southern coast of King William's
Land (which, to them would appear more like a
mainland or continent than Adelaide Peninsula
of which Point Ogle forms the north-east
boundary), and as the party may have attempted
to reach the Great Fish River by striking eastward along it, it is quite probable that instead

of pushing for the coast of Adelaide Peninsula, they followed the course described, and being too much exhausted to reach their object have perished. Whether their remains are to be found on either coast, it is obvious they were unable through want to reach the Great Fish River, and have perished. Moreover, it would require no great labour of the Esquimaux near the mouth of that stream to carry the traces found on them from those lands. The obstacles to be met in retreat would arise from the difficult nature of the ice contrasted with their feeble condition; being the spring of the year when they arrived on the north coast of King William's Land, the ice in Victoria as in Simpson Strait would be unbroken thereby, making travelling difficult. At this period may be observed the truth and simplicity of the Esquimaux statement in finding the remains of the party previous to the breaking up of the ice, thus proving distinctly they had great difficulties to encounter after quitting the north coast of King William's Land. Had they made that coast in the autumn they must have been favoured with open water in their retreat, but arriving in the spring or commencement of summer the route towards the continent would abound with difficulties, from the great labour attending travelling over ice covered with snow partly dissolved by the noon-day sun, their journey would be both long and tedious. To

view this question in its true light, we could not
expect a starving party to accomplish a retreat
from the north coast of King William's Land in
the face of the obstacles therein presented.   The
expedition under Mr. Anderson explored the
north-east coast of Adelaide Peninsula, but its
search was too confined to produce any beneficial
results.   Why its parties did not push their
search to the western coast of that Peninsula or
to the south coast of King William's Land is
difficult to say; were that impossible, why did
they not proceed eastward to the Esquimaux in
Pelly Bay, a visit to those tribes might have
been productive of different results to those
attained.   Retreat to Fort Churchill being open
as with Dr. Rae, there was a much greater
chance of being rewarded for their labour by
following that course than returning destitute of
information by the way they advanced. We should
have been spared all anxiety, every hope of success,
had the Hudson's Bay Company informed us
what their expedition of '55 was to do previous to
setting out; its barren effects are not attributable
to difficulties but to negligence.   At a late period
of the season and without interpreters it left
Fort Resolution.   It remained eight days on
the seat of search, and this, with all the pride
imaginable, was called a search for Franklin.
That company pocketed the sum of £2500, for
not only deluding this country, but for turning
into ridicule the sacred subject of Franklin's fate;

a blot will ever remain on its character in allowing many portions of land within reach of its settlements to remain unsearched for the lost navigators, when without difficulty it could complete all that was desired. Why did it suffer the coast between the Coppermine and Great Fish Rivers to remain unexplored after the seasons of '47—48, and why does it do so to this day ? an eight days' search was the least it could give to the man who had previously risked his life for an extension of its territories ; yet, rather than give a slight check to its selfish will, it would suffer ten years to pass away and after all make the British public pay dearly in mind and in pocket for that which actually had not the appearance of an intention.

Bringing the Hudson's Bay Company's disgraceful expedition of '55 to its wretched termination, it concludes the past search for Franklin, and giving close attention to a future search for the retreating party, we view the present prospects in the following light. The whole coast line of King William's Land is still unexplored ; the lands between the Coppermine and Great Fish Rivers are yet to be searched, while both shores of Peel Sound commencing at Dr. Rae's discoveries and extending north-ward to those of M. Bellot remain to be traver-sed ere the search is complete. It will be seen by a chart that the line of search is long and irregular ; we have a wide spread field before us

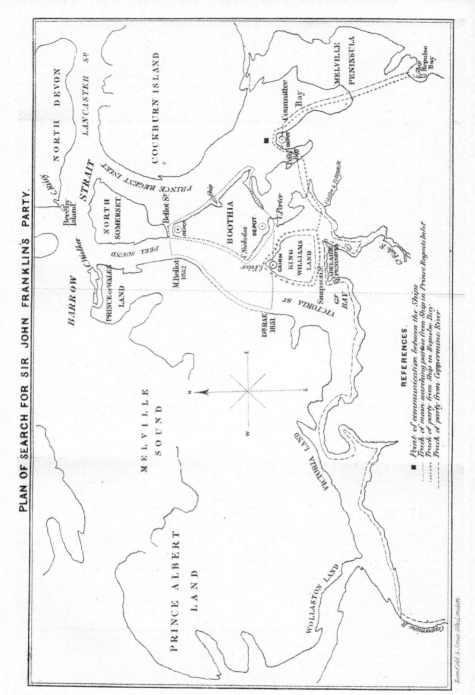

PLAN OF SEARCH FOR SIR JOHN FRANKLIN'S PARTY.

The material originally positioned here is too large for reproduction in this reissue. A PDF can be downloaded from the web address given on page iv of this book, by clicking on 'Resources Available'.

and a difficult route to reach it. In the absence
of open water ships become useless, therefore the
search must be conducted over the ice attached
to those lands by well organised boat parties ;
one great object is to facilitate those journeys by
removing the difficulties and by reducing the
labour attending them into as small a compass
as possible without any danger, rendering the
search withal as complete as can be desired,
and planning a search according to the position
of those lands upon which our attention is
fixed.

I place my views thus.—Let two small screw
steamers be prepared by the coming spring, and
under able commanders, with crews of about thirty
experienced voyagers each, proceed at once, one
to Repulse Bay and the other up Lancaster
Sound, and down the western shore of Prince
Regent's Inlet; first to Bellot Strait, leaving
a depot on its southern shore, then continue
down the inlet for a central position in the search.
At the same time let a small party descend the
Coppermine River, to carry the search eastward
to the Great Fish River. To make escape
certain to all engaged, the ship in Repulse Bay
should become the centre of retreat, as when
parties are in that bay, retreat to the settlements
in Hudson's Bay can be effected without great
danger. Two seasons will be required for the
work to be done by the ships, but the party

descending the Coppermine River will complete
its task in one.   It would at the earliest period
of the season be near the close of August when
the ship passing through Lancaster Sound
could secure a position on the western shore of
Prince Regent's Inlet, while it may be doubted
whether the vessel destined to Repulse Bay
could reach her quarters before that period of
the year.   The party from the Coppermine
River, after closely searching the lands between
it and the Great Fish River, should pause at
the entrance to the latter stream, to examine
the Esquimaux tribes around for traces or
information, and instead of retreating by the
way it advanced, must push eastward and
complete its journey to the ship in Repulse Bay.
And that vessel arriving too late in the season
to search the coast line of King William's Land,
should first direct a party up to the head of
Committee Bay, to open communication with
the men from Prince Regent's Inlet, and render,
if necessary, assistance to that returning from
the Coppermine River.   Pending these proceedings, and if time would permit, a select few
should be sent up the eastern coast of Melville Peninsula, in search of Esquimaux, from
whom important intelligence might be received.
The ship would then winter, and make every
preparation for the ensuing spring.   When
April arrived a well organised party should
leave to search the whole coast line of King

William's Land. After reaching the entrance to Castor and Pollux River, it should strike westward for the south-east point of that land. Arriving there, it divides itself thus :—One half go up its eastern coast, and the other along that of its southern, meeting together at Cape Felix, its north-west boundary, they erect a cairn, and then retreat to the depot fixed to the northward of Cape Porter; from that point to the depot at the head of Committee Bay, and southward to their ship. While this party was absent, another small one may be despatched from the ship up the west and northern coasts of Melville Peninsula in quest of Esquimaux. Another, similarly equipped, should be sent up the shores of Committee and Pelly Bays for the same object. Allowing three months and a half to complete the work by this ship, and if afloat or released from the ice, the return to England could be accomplished without delay. But if escape to the ship is impossible, let the crew retreat to the settlements in Hudson's Bay in time to secure a passage to England by that Company's ships. And now turning our attention to the ship in Prince Regent's Inlet. Immediately after reaching her destination a party must be despatched to form a depot at the head of Committee Bay, a distance of one hundred miles, and to open communication with the men from Repulse Bay. Having accomplished

G

this, and the lands around the ship being
explored for Esquimaux, they pass the winter
and make every preparation for the following
spring. April arriving, two parties should leave
the ship, the smallest going north and the
largest south, and across the lakes to the
westward to form a depot above Cape Porter.
If that position be too far from the ship, let it
be fixed at the head of the middle lake, as at
either point it must prove of great value to
the parties returning from King William's Land
and the western shore of Peel Sound. After
leaving the depot, the party must divide. Let
one half go up the western coast of Boothia,
to Cape Nickolai, and follow that coast northward to Bellot Strait, where it would find
relief from the depot left in that Strait
by the ship. The return journey could then
be made at leisure, while the other half should
trace the south-west coast of Boothia, from
Cape Porter southward to Castor and Pollux
River, after reaching which it must turn, and
taking a north-east track, arrive at the head
of Pelly Bay, and search the coast northward
for Esquimaux, returning to the ship by the
lake district. The smallest or northern party
leaving the ship in the spring, must push up
Prince Regent's Inlet, and if needful touch at
the depot in Bellot Strait. It should then
cross Peel Sound, and make its western shore
near M. Bellot's position in '52, after which

it can follow that coast southward to Dr. Rae's
position in '51 on the western shore of Victoria
Strait; turning to the eastward from that
point, it should make for Cape Felix, and then
on finding the cairn built by the Repulse Bay
party retreat direct to the depot northward of
Cape Porter, and thus to their ship; this duty
might be performed in three months and a half,
at the expiration of which they could return to
England. But should the release of the ship
appear hopeless, (as with Sir John Ross in 1832)
then, after a proportionate rest, her crew should
retreat south to the depot at the head of
Committee Bay, from thence to the ship or
depot left in Repulse Bay, and thus to the
settlements in time to secure with the others a
passage to England.

The precautionary measures to be adopted
are as follows. No searching party to leave
the ships unaccompanied by interpreters. The
ship for Repulse Bay shall first visit the settlements in Hudson's Bay and take therefrom
the necessary number of interpreters for both
ships. Those for Prince Regent's Inlet ought to
proceed with the first communicating party from
Repulse Bay, and on meeting the men from
Prince Regent's Inlet go with them northward to their ship. Should the crew in Prince
Regent's Inlet be compelled to retreat, the hope
of meeting whalers by pushing north to Barrow
Strait must not be entertained, and if the ships are

icebound for a season, it may be prudent to leave
a sufficient crew aboard them with the hope
of resuming them in the following season.
Communication ought to be strictly attended
to, and above all let there be sealed orders
given; each officer should clearly understand
the points at which relief or information may
be obtained, so that if his party require
either he may know where it is to be found.
In a word the whole plan of search should be
settled previous to quitting England.

Attention must also be given to the Esquimaux tribes, as dogs and sledges and other valuable assistance may be purchased from them.
The above plan will be found to contain
all that is necessary for an effectual search
without great danger to those engaged, and
without enormous expense, the cost of main-
taining a government vessel with a crew of
sixty men, divided thus, thirty for the ship in
Prince Regent's Inlet, twenty for that in Repulse
Bay, and ten for the party descending the
Coppermine River, would complete the search
to the satisfaction of Great Britain and
the world in general; whereas to despatch
one ship or party to explore that long and
difficult line of coast, and to thoroughly examine
the Esquimaux tribes, would fall far short of ob-
taining the great object in view. A partial
search might find traces and yet leave us still in
doubt, but if the lands named be explored as

recommended, the search will then, and not till then, be complete. Success, that much desired object, must reward us one way or other, for if the combined searching parties failed to discover the documents or remains of the party that have perished, their explorations would clearly prove whether Franklin's ships had been wrecked or detained either in Victoria Strait or Peel Sound. No attempt to push ships on search through Peel Sound should be made, as from the impenetrable nature of the ice within it every such attempt must end in disappointment. That it will be attempted is probable, but that it will succeed is utterly impossible ; and as it is certain that the missing ships have been wrecked and their crews have perished by the difficulties and dangers of Peel Sound, why send a vessel on search through the same channel, if they could overcome the skill of Franklin and his officers with a crew of one hundred and thirty-five men, how indeed are others on search to escape them? I advocate a future search for documents, by which the position of the remaining men may be known, but the public insists on a search of Peel Sound for the ships of Franklin. I consider another search well rewarded by finding the papers and remains of the party that have perished, yet the world will be sadly disappointed if the missing ships are not found and the whole mystery revealed. It is therefore against this immeasurable confidence

that we ought to be guarded; England has
already been too far misled in this difficult and
deeply interesting subject, and if either its
learned or labouring classes still maintain the
belief that the lost ships were wrecked in Peel
Sound, they are supporting a view without the
slightest foundation, and cherishing a hope
which by the balance of reason can never be
realized. Let the public therefore be on its
guard against the results of a future search,
lest while indulging too much confidence, its
powers of penetration are hurled with irresis-
tible force into the lowest depths of obscurity,
for should the search of Victoria Strait and
Peel Sound be accomplished, and no traces of
the missing ships be discovered, not only
will a fearful justice overtake its frail speculations, but the curtain about to be so suddenly lifted will fall again with tenfold darkness over the mysterious fate of our countrymen, sealing all further hope in a gloom only
to be rivalled by the horrors of their dungeon.

It is truly lamentable to think that all the
learning, talent, and science of this country
were unable to rescue the lives of those brave
men, but what a profound silence will reign
over the land respecting their fate, when the
world can no longer speculate on their woes,
their death, nor even the scenes of their sufferings, when the mind is placed beyond the
limits of calculation and all its inventive
powers are brought to a stand, time alone that

waits for no man, then must reveal the Franklin mystery.

A review of the past brings to our notice another report seriously engaging public attention; in the spring of 1855, a statement appeared from one Thomas Mistigan, or Mastitukwin, who accompanied Dr. Rae on his interesting voyage in '54, the purport of which was, that Sir John Franklin and his party are dead, but perhaps one or two of the men may be still alive and with the Esquimaux. Sir John's watch, all in pieces, with his silver spoons, knives and forks, were found. The ship was a great godsend to these people; they now all having good sledges, spears, canoes, &c., of oak wood. I should not have deemed this report worthy of notice, had it not been commented upon in the following terms by the press. " Such are the words of Masti-tukwin's narrative as detailed to the Revd. Thomas Hurlbert, of Rossville Mission, Hudson's Bay. They are entitled to credence because the narrator is a native of the country, acquainted with the language, and could have no object in making a false statement. The various imple-ments made of oak, which were seen in the Esquimaux encampment, prove that they must have had access to at least one of the ships of the missing expedition.

Why not, scorning to affect a greater insight into this question than others, I ask were the services of Thomas Mistigan, if he possessed a better knowledge of the Esqui-

maux language than did Ooligbuck, (Dr. Rae's
interpreter,) not accepted as interpreter to that
expedition, and if his report was entitled to credence because he is a native of the country, acquainted with the language, and could have no
object in making a false statement, surely the
statements of Ooligbuck, also a native of the country, possessing as good a knowledge of the language, are equally worthy of credence. What motive had the interpreter who accompanied Sir John
Ross in 1850 in sustaining the vile report of the
murder of Franklin's crews near the top of
Baffin's Bay by a tribe of savage Esquimaux?
I have no desire to accuse Mistigan of falsehood,
yet in dwelling on the remarks made on his
statement by the press, we cannot help feeling a
little annoyed at their inconsistency; Franklin's
watch being found broken into various pieces, how
did the Esquimaux know that it belonged to him?
Could its maker much less any of those tribes
have identified those mutilated fragments? and
when Mistigan did not see the good sledges,
spears, and canoes in the hands of Esquimaux,
how was the nature of the wood identified?
Are we to understand from the press, that boats
and sledges are called implements, or must we
remain in ignorance of what was seen by Mistigan? It is possible he may have been endowed
with the gift of second sight.

But of the wood work seen with the Esquimaux by Dr. Rae's party in '54, the following
report made by that traveller and published by him

in the *Times* of December 15th, 1856, gives a
striking description. " In 1854 the Esquimaux I
met with in the same localities as in 1846 and '47
had very few wood sledges, and those were extremely old and much worn, some of the sledges
were made of bone, but the majority were of
musk ox skin folded up on a little wet moss
or mud in the form of a sledge runner,
and then frozen. These last are never used
when the Esquimaux can get wood, as in
the spring, (at which season the natives travel
most) they are thawed and put out of shape
by the heat of the midday sun. In 1847
wood was not in great demand by the natives
because they had an ample supply for all their
wants, from the wreck of the Victory left by Sir
John Ross in 1832 in Felix Harbour. But in
1854 a small piece sufficient for a spear handle
was valued more highly than a large dagger.
The conclusion I came to was that if Franklin's
ships or one of them had been found by the
Esquimaux, they would have been equally well
supplied in 1854 as they were in 1347." I quote
Dr. Rae's report not as from one of high authority, but merely to show what was seen of wood
kind by his party in the possession of the Esquimaux; yet, assuming experience to be authority, it comes from one of the highest
standing. My remarks on the second Esquimaux narrative being brought to a close,
I shall now add a few words touching the

advantages which experience has been to this very interesting subject. Few venture an opinion upon it without producing the view of some eminent man as their authority; and then they are led away by the impression that he must be correct, in fact we are told he cannot be wrong, and in return deserve the lash for daring to presume. Let science wage its own great course like the glorious orb of heaven, or the lustre of experience secure for man the worship. of his race, but let neither assume that garb of deceit which was never intended to adorn such noble qualifications. Why are the opinions of one experienced officer or the scientific authority of another, cited as affecting the mysterious fate of Franklin, when it has for the past ten years held at naught the powers of them all? If a thorough knowledge of the Esquimaux or a long experience in the Arctic regions can benefit in any way this melancholy chapter, let the wondrous line of ethnologists, with the most celebrated Arctic navigators, advance, and as a splendid phalanx prove their right to supremacy over other classes. With due respect to science as to experience, I humbly admit their claims on all but every subject. Yet that either is entitled to authority in this painful question, I am prepared to deny, if necessary, with my last breath; though we are not confounded we may well be surprised that the talent of the press should be so far misled as to trumpet Mistigan's report throughout the king-

dom as the awful fate of Sir John Franklin,
holding it up to public gaze as if it alone
had exposed the whole mystery: had it revealed
the fact of a ship being previously wrecked in
the locality where that report arose, the people
would have been enlightened as to its truth,
instead of being led blindfolded by that which
received no attention from those who thought
fit to give it publication. It was really so
much like the blind leading the blind that a
celebrated picture no longer shrinks from view.

After its very active campaign against the
missing expedition it ill becomes us to remain
in sullen silence. The influence of the press is
an acknowledged truth by all the world, and,
moreover, is considered by foreign powers to be
the strong unfettered arm of the British people.
As its enchanting pen, therefore, renders important services to the eminent statesmen or distinguished parties in the political strife of this
country, it certainly does seem more than
strange that it has not been employed in clearing
up this national mystery. If through want of
foresight it was unable to do so it should
not have deterred others from making the
attempt, nor have placed such unbounded
confidence in that which was doubtful.
When the Esquimaux narrative became known
in 1854, it plied its pen with unusual
vigour, though not to disclose its real nature, but to add horror to horror, dark-

ness to darkness, by giving colour to every un-
just surmise, and deadening all further affection
of the public towards the long lost navigators.

On the 27th of November 1856 the *Times*
sent forth a leading article against a further
search in language that betrays a burning desire
to conceal the want of knowledge, while it
makes manifest the troubles of a mind unable
at all times to withstand the inroads of despon-
dency. The subjoined is its contents. "Another
expedition in search of Sir John Franklin is now
meditated, and while it is yet time we would
invoke the aid of public opinion to put a stop at
once to so outrageous a proceeding; we cannot
of course prevent individuals from doing whatever they may please. If a party of gentlemen
choose to sail a brig to the centre of the Atlantic
and there agree to scuttle her and go down in a
friendly manner together, who shall stop them?
We do, however, most vehemently protest
against the extension of any assistance from the
public funds or from the public establishments
to so preposterous a scheme as another expedition
in search of Sir John Franklin's relics. The
proposition was again brought forward on
Monday evening at a meeting of the Geographical
Society. Lieutenant Pim on that occasion read
his outline of a plan for a further search after
the missing expedition under Sir John Franklin.
Nothing of course can be made to appear more
simple on paper or more easy of accomplishment

than such a design. If we had lost all recollection of former years and former expeditions of the like kind we might almost be tempted to add faith to the words of the speaker or of the writer; we cannot, however, but remember that just the same kind of thing was said or written years ago, as each fresh expedition was planned, and in due course was despatched to the frost region. Nothing was more easy than to sail to the extreme eastern point of that great inlet in which Franklin had disappeared; or up this sound to the northward, or that arm of the sea to the southward, or round by Behring's Straits, or in any of half a dozen directions; most of these suggestions were followed, and we know what came of it. Some of the expeditionary ships were seized in fields of ice and hurled back on the rocky coast, others for a long time were lost to human knowledge. Ship was despatched after ship and expedition after expedition, until finally, by a miracle almost, the crews of the vessels were withdrawn; the vessels themselves being abandoned, jammed hard and firm in the ice. It is not our business in the course of these few remarks to discuss any results that have arisen from these exertions and sacrifices save two; in the first place Franklin and his unfortunate companions are dead long since (human frailty), that much we know from the relics which Dr. Rae brought home; and secondly, bitter experience has told us that these ice expeditions, however speciously they may be introduced to public notice, invariably terminate in the most terrible anxieties and in disappointment which may well be looked on as complete when we compare the results realized with the expeditions formed and the promises held out. We are really so sick of the subject that we do not care to follow Lieutenant Pim and Sir Roderick Murchison into their discussions as to the best method of reaching the spot where some of Franklin's relics may still be found.

"It is gratifying to find from Sir Roderick Murchison's observations that the government have not yet committed themselves to this frantic scheme. Sir Roderick is reported to have said if the government would not send out an expedition, he was authorized to state that that noble-minded woman, Lady Franklin, although there might be no chance of saving any one living man, had determined to send out another expedition on her own account to those regions. We trust Lady Franklin may be better advised, but of course it is not within our province to make any remark upon the proceedings of private persons. If the scientific gentlemen wish for another expedition let them man the ships in their own proper persons, and prove that they do not shrink from the perils to which they would expose others. The present government or any government will be most deeply to blame if they give any kind of encouragement to so hazardous and useless a proceeding." Leaving posterity to judge on the wisdom of that production, I also append the most interesting part of a second article, dated December 2nd, '56, called forth by the cry of indignation, which greeted the advent of the first. "It is with great reluctance that we call public opinion to the aid of the government in opposition to the views of so many gentlemen of high character and great ability. We for our part are perfectly convinced that Sir John Franklin, who on the 26th of May 1845 sailed from Sheerness with the Erebus and Terror, has long since gone to his account, he, Captain Crozier, and all the officers and men under their command. The last that was known of them previous to the discoveries of the relics by Dr. Rae, was that they spent the winter of 1845—46 at a particular spot. Yes, the only certain fact known about Franklin and his friends is that precisely eleven years ago, reckoning from the present month of December, they were moving about and living in a small cove between Cape Riley and Beechy Island facing Lancaster Sound. But eleven years have elapsed since then, and if the length of time, the inhospitable character of the regions in which they were cast away, and the recent discovery of their relics be not sufficient to satisfy any dispassionate enquirer that our unfortunate fellow countrymen have long since ceased to be numbered among the living, his mind must be very differently constituted from our own. Upon this point we have nothing more to say, but that if any one really still holds to the opinion that Franklin is alive, or of course one of his followers, we can well understand that he should advocate the propriety of further re-search. We who are absolutely of the other opinion say, that such further re-search would be perilous to the living, and useless to the dead."

In October '54 the *Times*, with an amount of candour rarely visible, acknowledged its inability to penetrate the mystery, but lately it has felt a deep-rooted interest in stopping all further search for those brave men, the reason why is of course better known to its editor than to ourselves ; still if we could indulge the hope that he would justly expose the subject, we might without loss of dignity stoop to inform him of its secrets. But as his acknowledgement of 1854 confirms the truth of his inability, and while his late extra-ordinary conduct mocks the name of justice, we shall better profit by saving pen and paper, and been spared the reflection of having spoken an unknown language. In the event of submission a slight effort would prove the cause of his sickness of the question, and the reason why, those who hold a contrary view have minds differently constituted from his own. Has the *Times* already forgotten the lesson it received on Kossuth's first visit to London ? for it

then barely managed to escape the last lash of
public vengeance; the executioner, it is true, was
alone wanting to complete the interesting cere-
mony; whether that event arose from a difference
of constitution between the public mind and that
of the *Times* editor is of course best known to
the public; but why does the *Times* lose sight
of this very difference by speaking with a morbid
certainty on the fate of Franklin? does it wish
to stop all further search with the hope of con-
cealing its own ignorance, or has it received a
certain sum for so doing. Why not at once disclose the fact, and no longer delude the public.
On the 28th of October '54, the *Examiner* be-
gan in the following strain. "There is no longer
any doubt of the melancholy death of Sir John
Franklin and his companions. When we discussed the subject in this journal at the close of
1849, we urged the necessity of then making
a final effort, and considering that the chances
would not warrant the risk of another expedition,
we held that it should have been planned on
such a scale, as completely to scour the track,
both by land and sea, in which the clearest
judgments might see the probabilities of success.
More than two years had then passed beyond the
time to which the ships were victualled, and we
believed it to be our last gleam of rational hope.
It is now proved to have been so (delightful
prophecy). Again, January 12th, 1856, Dr.
Rae had understood the Esquimaux to mean

H

Montreal Island and Point Ogle near it as the
places where the white men perished in 1850.
The recent search has determined the locality
beyond disupte (a startling revelation). The circulation of a falsehood for the condemnation of
the unfortunate, is a crime placed far beyond the
pale of redemption : it is notoriously false that
more than two years had passed from the time
to which the missing ships were victualled, when
in '49 the *Examiner* made that statement, and
though quite heedless as to the truth of its
publications, it remained as careless of their results.   In Franklin's despatch dated Whale Fish
Island, July 12th, 1845, as in the report made
by Lieutenant Griffiths, commander of the
transport accompanying the missing ships to
those islands, both agree that the ships had on
board when leaving those islands July 13th, '45,
stores and provisions of every description for
three entire years from that date, consequently,
on full allowance they would serve until July 13th,
48, so that the *Examiner's* statement was not
only false, but as base as it was false, must it
urge a final effort in '49, when Franklin's first
winter quarters remained undiscovered. Was the
last search necessary because Sir James Ross
was unsuccessful. If he violated the trust reposed
in him by the nation, was the press to do the
same ?   In '49 the chances would not warrant
the risk of another expedition, it was our last
gleam of rational hope, and in '54, it is now

proved to have been so. Such was the address
made to this country at the time when its people
were tortured by a story, the horrors of which
held them in suspense and awe; those were the
impious sentiments teeming with frantic despair
which we all had the mortification to hear
without a protestation, and why? because they
came from the press that must rule us. As a
further repetition of its shameless fabrications
will but excite a feeling of horror, I will close the
criminal list by a short instance well deserving a
place in future history. In August 1856 the
United Service Gazette contained a paragraph
entitled ' Another Arctic Expedition ' wherein it
says :—

"A report is again current that another expedition, to be placed in command of Captain
Inglefield, is to be despatched to the Arctic
regions, in the hope of brushing away some of
the cobwebs which have of late gathered thickly
around the brains of certain savans of the different learned societies! we protest in the name of
common sense and common humanity against
this contemplated waste of the resources of the
country and the risk of the lives of our adventurous tars." The press undoubtedly believes
that in giving publicity to these cruel maledic-
tions, it is expressing the opinions of the country,
but however much it may control the people
they cannot every day applaud such depraved
barbarity; it may find before long that it is

much better to remain silent on a subject of
which it knows nothing than to expose itself to
an eternal disgrace, which a revelation of the
Franklin mystery would assuredly entail on it.
Throughout its reports we discern a speedy intention of ridding itself of a subject it never
strove to unravel, and which, for want of attention, or through stubborn ignorance, it gave
up as hopeless; it tolled their death knell, long
ere they entered on the scenes of their sufferings,
and without an attempt in 1854 to bring the
Esquimaux narrative to a reasonable light, it
rushed with headstrong haste to swell the terrors
of that awful story; it gloried in the prophecy
of their miserable end; and after a visionary
glance at the mystery, without indulging to ex-
cess its powers of penetration, it joined the
vast cataract of despair to plunge the fate of
our unfortunate countrymen into the gulf of
oblivion. Did it forget that Nero fiddled while
Rome was burning, or had it a peculiar desire
only to imitate that immortal scene? which of the
two is doubtful. But from its conduct we can
extract the sorrowful reflection that the country
who sent those ill-fated men will from example
look on their mysterious fate as a passive specta-
tor suffering their remains to be undiscovered
and unburied, and probably believing the time
is come when the whole subject of their untimely
end must sink without hope into the silence of
everlasting sleep; and as no other doubt can arise

but that the alluring majesty of the press will in future implore the public in the name of common sense and common humanity, to stop all further search for those brave men, we are left merely to bid it adieu with the same disregard it has so long shown to life and to honour.

CHAPTER III.

In the prosecution of our subject I append a
few general remarks on the present condition of
the mystery ; the first is, the entire absence of
cylinders, balloons, or papers from balloons
belonging to the missing expedition.   It is a
remarkable circumstance that though nearly
twelve years have expired since its departure,
but one cylinder has been found, and that in the
same waters to which it was consigned in '45,
namely, Baffin's Bay ; the only just decision to be
formed thereon, is, that its position is both difficult and distant; it does not seem probable that
Franklin put cylinders into Barrow Strait in '46
when about to quit Beechey Island, as the despatches left at that island would better suit the
purpose, while, if he did so when running to the
westward of Cape Lady Franklin, the westerly
set of the current beyond that cape would prove
an effectual bar against their appearance in
Barrow Strait or Baffin's Bay.

Of the traces found, supposed to belong to the missing ships, let us speak. In 1853 Captain Collinson found part of a door or doorframe, attached to which was a hasp, bearing the broad arrow, or British Government mark, together with a piece of galvanised iron, in possession of the Esquimaux around Cambridge Bay. In 1851 Dr. Rae, when traversing the western shore of Victoria Strait, found part of a boat's mast, also a piece of wood said to be a part of a ship's stanchion. The iron affording no clue whatever we pass to the other traces, and acknowledge that the hasp found had belonged to this Government, but whether it had been attached to a ship, a boat, or a hut, is as difficult to say, as whether it had belonged to Franklin. The wood, and part of boats mast, found by Dr. Rae on the track of the retreating party, leave no doubt of their having been left by it; yet as there is no certainty as to this wood being part of a ship's stanchion, we cannot say whether it belonged to a ship, or if it was of any service to the party. These feeble traces, if such they may be called, appear somewhat in the same light as the piece of English elm, found floating in Wellington Channel by the searching parties in '50. But without carrying the same weight as that trace, the wood was burnt at one end, which leads to the opinion that it had been used as a fire by the retreating party, to attract the attention of

searching parties in the dark months while in
the neighbourhood of Beechey Island. To follow
any of these further would lead to no results,
for unless we have a foundation on facts or circumstances, we cannot form a correct view.
Declining, therefore, lest I should be in pursuit of
a phantom always on the wing, I turn with
attention to the absence of traces connecting
the lost ships. It is a fact upon which too much
stress cannot be laid, that every article found by
Dr. Rae and Mr. Anderson goes no further than
to show that they had belonged to a boat party,
and excepting every trace in one view, a party
such as that seen by the Esquimaux in 1850,
could, without difficulty, carry all that was
found.

It is satisfactory to know that in the statement
made by Dr. Rae, in that of Mr. Anderson, as in
the report lately brought home by Captain
Penny, all are silent on the position of Franklin's
ships. The Esquimaux seen on Boothia, Victoria
Land, and on the Great Fish River, when asked
the direct question if they had seen the ships,
answered in the negative, and without placing
any reliance on their statement, its truth is
powerfully apparent by the absence of traces
connecting the ships with them. Had they informed us otherwise, the absence of such traces
on them would have proved their assertion false.
That two ships were detained or wrecked in a
locality infested by tribes of wandering Esqui-

maux, and should remain for ten years without being seen by them, is an idea far too absurd to be true. To allay further doubt upon this subject, one question is necessary. When the Esquimaux first saw the white men on the coast of King William's Land, and hearing they had left their ships in the ice, seeing at the same time the direction from which they were advancing, would they not have set off in quest of them? We are entitled to believe that those tribes have traversed Peel Sound and Victoria Strait in every direction for the missing ships, but their search being unsuccessful, hence the absence of traces of them. That they were in that position was a question to be discussed in '47 and '48, but not afterwards, as the great search that followed those seasons, the long lapse of time and the total absence of tidings, were surely sufficient to convince the world of its bad judgment. Had any consideration been given to those truths, the public would not have remained long in a state of ignorance concerning the mystery. The warning voice of caution called aloud in the results of Mr. Anderson's voyage, still, like Jehu, it drove on, and became at length fixed on the one hundred and fifteen unexplored miles in Peel Sound. The great catastrophe, with a complete history of the discoveries, adventures, and misfortunes of those one hundred and thirty-five men, led by able officers, must and will be found in the narrow confines of that distance.

Careful of order we ask, was the party seen in
'50 by the Esquimaux the last survivors of the
missing crews? If so, why did they not retreat
to Fury Beach, instead of pushing in a starving
condition towards the hunting grounds and the
settlements? What induced them to face death
but the view of getting communication and
sending relief to those left behind with the ships?
In their journey south, through Peel Sound,
Fury Beach lay within easy reach, still it was
forsaken. A bare existence awaited them at
that place, and a death march presented itself in
the route through Peel Sound; had they entertained any hope of finding intelligence of ships
after reaching Cape Walker, it would concentrate
on Fury Beach, as it was the only place where
provisions could be found, which circumstance
would render it a position likely to be visited by
searching parties. The absence of the retreating party from it exhibits the haste to get communication, while it indicates the absence of all
hopes of receiving succour from ships after it
had been to Cape Walker. Many will speak
of a second party attempting a retreat from the
ships, but the objections to that view is but one
route being open for retreat, and the first party
having consumed the stores left at the junction
of Jones' Sound with Wellington Channel.
When they were gone Franklin knew that without a depot in the line of retreat, the attempt
would be too hazardous, which, with the expec-

tation that the first party would make known
his position, would prevent a second attempt
being made, while the heavy nature of the
ice to the westward of Baring and Melville Islands
would render escape to the continent in that
direction impossible.

In the contemplation of a future search we
are impelled by reason, humanity, and justice
to do that which is no more than our duty to the
long lost Arctic heroes; therefore I appeal to the
civilized world by the strongest dictates of
reason, through every humane motive, and by
all the ties of friendship pertaining to mankind,
to arouse from its present slumber and prosecute
the search until it is successful; as for this
age, it will risk its reputation by suffering the
mystery to die away in its present form; for
the great neglect, the mismanaged search, and
lastly the cruel silence with which it has been
treated, will be handed down to posterity as the
degradation of these times. The future historian
will record the fate of Franklin as an instance
of the imbecility of Great Britain; whilst
generations to come will speak of it in amazement; it will pass on to the great period of time
and be called the legend of the nineteenth
century. Let us then shake off this impending
chastisement by a future and proper search, as
there is not only miles of traces to be discovered
but hundreds of miles, from the time they left
Beechey Island in '46 until the retreat in '49—

50 will verify my statement. There is every
probability of many of the crew still living; the
dark curtain has yet to be lifted; all in fact
remains to be known.   Should the government
of this country turn a deaf ear to their cries,
farewell to our national honour, farewell now
and for ever to all hopes of ascertaining the
fate of our countrymen.   The stern and icy
feelings of England will then reign triumphant;
that cold spirit which distinguishes her from
other nations and sacrifices day by day some
one of her neglected but talented sons will
then rule supreme over the fate of the gallant
Sir John Franklin.

An instance of the probability of papers being
still in existence amongst the Esquimaux, is
seen by Dr. Rae in '54 finding on them part of
a book called the "Student's Manual."   It is
singular that those tribes should preserve this
book that was of no value to them.   Had they
not taken a peculiar interest in its preservation
it would not have been found in '54.   The only
interest they could have in exercising this care is
clearly in favour of the white men, who may
have given their papers to the Esquimaux to
preserve until those tribes met searching parties;
however this may be papers were found in '54
and may be in existence to this day, and if
diligently sought for amongst the Esquimaux be
recovered.   In the book found was a leaf marked
or doubled, which had evidently fixed the

attention of its reader ; the part most prominent
appears to have been studied by one whose
worldly position was hopeless. The importance
attached bespeaks the sentiments of a mind fully
reposed in the works of its Creator ; it reads
thus :—

" Are you not afraid to die? "

" No."

" Why does the uncertainty of another state
give you no concern ? "

" Because God has said to me fear not, when
thou passest through the waters I will be with
thee, and through the rivers they shall not
overflow thee."

This beautiful passage breathes throughout
a fervid resignation, its spiritual brightness
impresses the mind with emotion, as it calls to
our sad recollection that solemn scene when the
feeble spirits of the exhausted party sunk in
silence from their fragile forms, though not with
the grandeur of the sun's bright setting rays,
but like the faint shadow of the pale moon
sorrowfully setting behind a dark cloud. It
reveals the same Christian tenderness as the
epithets left by Franklin over the graves of his
men at Beechey Island. Here his character
stands out in bold relief and wins our admira-
tion ; it appears exceedingly grand when
he was about to pass from the known to
the unknown world, that he should adorn the
last resting places of his bereaved companions

with the finest effusions of his own great soul;
not knowing whether his own remains would
find a sepulchre.

The question deferred to this period was that
of Franklin having in '46 turned his back to
the passage with the intention of returning to
England.   If that report is worth a refutation,
and while his character deserves the highest
praise, a few words in his behalf from one ever
ready to assist the heroes of his country may
not be considered out of place.   His character
stood all but alone in zeal, bold daring, and in
enterprise, for a man to retain at the advanced
age of sixty all the boldness and energy of youth,
singularly blended with the lofty qualities of
religion, is a combination rarely found in one
individual; with a mind that had overcome the
greatest of difficulties, was a heart as generous
as it was brave.   Did the founders of that report
forget they were speaking of a hero of Copenha-
gen and Trafalgar, and one who was brought up
from boyhood to discovery? Is this the man who
in 1818 sailed to discover a passage north-east
of Spitzbergen, and when his senior's ship was
disabled requested to prosecute that perilous path
alone.   Is this the same Franklin who in 1821
—26 led with success under sufferings of an
awful description, two of the most daring boat
expeditions that ever left this country.   And is
this he who after a long and useful life strongly
chequered by misfortunes left the shores of his

native land to seek the north-west passage ; to suffer in consequence or miserably to die. Such were the deeds of Franklin ; this is the character of the man now lost to the world, in the wild northern wastes of eternal snow. Is calumny England's reward to a devoted hero, and cold neglect a just tribute to her gallant sons ? Is this all they are to receive for seeking their country's glory? Was it for this they traversed lands unknown ? We may regret many unfortunate events connected with their fate ; but none more than this, that they had not the chance of turning their backs to the passage as the expeditions on search have done ; all were favoured with that good fortune but Sir John Franklin. In reference to the number of men left with the ships in '49, if we deduct forty (the number comprising the retreating party) from a hundred and thirty-five Franklin took from Beechey Island in '46, he had ninety-five left, and allowing five deaths a year (which is beyond the average mortality of ordinary Arctic expeditions) in '49 there remained eighty men whose fate must remain a very doubtful question. Having no hope of finding Franklin with the retreating party of '49, my conclusions are drawn : from his advanced age and disposition he would on no consideration leave the remaining and sickly portion of his crews behind, he would not lead them into those distant parts and there

desert them.   If ever he is found he will be with
the ships or near their position.   We shall see
him again as in 1821 diffusing around the
faint and dying forms of his companions the
same sympathy of his own Christian soul.
As to the determination he could come to
respecting the fate of the retreating party it is
beyond the powers of mankind to conceive.
He might believe they had perished through
want in seeking relief, or that a sad calamity
had befallen them before they could give an
alarm ; but he would be unable to bring himself
to the extraordinary conclusion that they had
retreated to the continent without being seen
living or dead.   He would still hold if they had
perished their remains would be found and the
position of his ships revealed. This is a thought
we cannot entertain without repeating it to memory, did the lives of the faithful party pass away with
the reflection still lingering over them that they
had never once been searched for.   After being
absent five years they visited places where succour
should have been and found none, therefore it must
have gone with them to the grave that they had
been forsaken in the midst of their distress, as
they found not a trace or mark to counteract the
bitterness of that sad thought.   Here their cruel
fate strikes terror to the imagination ; they did
not succumb without a struggle, but sunk into
eternal repose exhausted by excessive toil, by
hunger, and privations indescribable, brought on

by a journey unprecedented in the progress of discovery; and which for boldness, disappointments, and unflinching endurance can never be surpassed. How well they laboured in a noble cause; every effort made was worthy of such heroes. Had this country displayed but half the zeal for their rescue that they did for their companions, they would not have been driven to such fatal extremes, but have been spared the belief that they had toiled in vain, and that the only cries of mourning over the lonely graves would be the loud murmurs of the northern blasts.

In returning to the fate of Franklin and the men left in the ships in 1849 we cannot determine the date of their death, as all depends on the produce of those parts in which they are imprisoned. On half allowance, their provisions would serve until the autumn of 1850, and if they were anything like successful in hunting or fishing, we lose all calculation. There is every likelihood of their taking deer, bears, musk-oxen, birds, and fish; when those could not be obtained, the wallruss, seals, and whales, could be made the means of supporting life, and that part of the Arctic regions where those are not found is at present unknown to mankind, consequently, any speculation upon the date of their death would amount to presumption, it being placed far beyond the limits of our understanding. For my own part, I doubt not that if ever their fate

I

is known the protracted period to which they
survived will create more astonishment than any
other part of the mystery.

That every stratagem was adopted to prolong
existence, the character of Franklin in former
voyages is a sufficient guarantee ; and when
combining his experience with the skill of his
officers, we at once discern the material necessary
for a long and desperate struggle ; as month by
month in season past and year rolled over year
they would stretch their ever anxious sight
across the wild expanse by which they were
surrounded.   But alas! to meet the dismal
prospects of the past, in all their wanderings
the same unchangeable horizon appeared to view.
Phantom ships no doubt oft-times disturbed their
troubled thoughts ; visions no sooner formed
than as soon would vanish. Thoughts mingling
the bright ray of hope with the darkness of
despair. I can imagine that forlorn band
ascending some lonely height, and aided by the
Arctic summer's never setting sun rivet their
gaze on the distant horizon in the hope of that
succour which was not to reach them—in a
vain search for that object they were destined
never to behold : and when the sun in autumn
set down o'er their trackless path, the joy with
which they had welcomed its appearance would
give way to the ravings of despair, as the dark
winter approached throwing its solitude with
awful effect around their icy prison. This would

continue season after season, until misery
succeeded misery, and the last ray of hope had
expired. Here they find themselves doomed to
end their lives on the scenes of their suffering
in a wild and dreary waste, ruled by silence long
and deep. Leaving our judgment now in repose,
and as wisdom forbears a further advance, we
must conclude with the last view of a subject
forming a painfully interesting chapter in
England's history. It is the loss of the whole
expedition.

When alluding to death, we touch on the
greatest of calamities; and in the grave of
Franklin must bury all remembrance of the
missing navigators; let us then speak of his
death as that of a great man : for in discovery
he ranked with the leading navigators. Numerous deeds of daring crowned him with the title
of a hero, while long and painful suffering gave
to his name the brand of immortality; embol-
dened by success, he made the fatal north-west
passage the pole star of his existence. In
bygone days that star arose in brilliant majesty
and scarce had climbed to its meridian splendour
ere its dazzling progress was arrested by the
fatal results of this undertaking.

And when chained on the verge of a lone
Arctic grave he beheld it decline in solemn
grandeur over the clouded horizon of his fate,
the parting shades of life's closing day calmly
gives place to the dark night of death : as his

gallant spirit sinks within him he forgets his distant home and country, and lifts his eyes toward the haven of his rest to seek protection in the bosom of His Maker; the last ebbing wave of life being hushed into silence, the pall of death closes mournfully over a life of perils, sufferings, and misfortunes, and a life once lit up by a conflagration of glory.

THE END.

For EU product safety concerns, contact us at Calle de José Abascal, 56–1°,
28003 Madrid, Spain or eugpsr@cambridge.org.

www.ingramcontent.com/pod-product-compliance
Ingram Content Group UK Ltd.
Pitfield, Milton Keynes, MK11 3LW, UK
UKHW012338130625
459647UK00009B/366